Writing Stories

The Nuts and Bolts of Writing Fiction

Ken Lewis

Detselig Enterprises Ltd.

Calgary, Alberta, Canada

Writing Stories
© 1996 Ken Lewis

Canadian Cataloguing in Publication Data

Lewis, Ken, 1925-
   Writing Stories

ISBN 1-55059-133-9

1. Fiction—Technique.   I. Title
PN3355.L48   1996   808.3   C96-910157-0

Detselig Enterprises Ltd.
210-1220 Kensington Rd. N.W.
Calgary, AB, T2N 3P5

Detselig Enterprises Ltd. appreciates the financial support for our 1996 publishing program, provided by the Department of Canadian Heritage and the Alberta Foundation for the Arts, a beneficiary of the Lottery Fund of the Government of Alberta.

Printed in Canada
ISBN 1-55059-133-9
SAN 115-0324

To my wife, Patricia, my best critic, my best friend and my best cheerleader.

And to all my hundreds of writing students who contributed in ways they never suspected.

Special thanks to my editor Terry Steward, whose comments and suggestions were always right on. And to the always helpful Jennifer Jolly, manager of We Can Copy.

CONTENTS

*Abstracting only the significant events and
organizing them into a meaningful significance
constitutes the storyteller's art.*
— S. I. Hayakawa

Ken Lewis in his Mexican office some years ago (note the technology).

Introduction

Successful writers are great readers. This book on the craft of story writing is no substitute for that enjoyable and beneficial activity, but it will give you the opportunity to learn the ABCs of story writing, while enriching your analytical powers so reading will more directly improve your writing.

Stories have a form. Stories contain certain universal elements. And stories have common writing techniques. From this book you can learn the form, discover the elements that all stories have in common and develop successful writing techniques.

I would be the first to admit successful story writing is an art. But it is first a craft. This book can help you learn the craft, and perhaps point the way toward the art.

Stories are the basic ingredient of writing whether it be a novel, short story, memoir, biography, history or even journalism. Successful writers have learned the fundamental principles of the story. Some have learned them from teachers or from textbooks. Others have absorbed them, either consciously or subconsciously, while reading.

From this book, you can learn these fundamentals, learn to recognize them in the writing of others and learn to apply them in your own writing. The story, like the wheel, does not need re-inventing.

This book is the result of my reading and a lengthy career as a journalist, author, reviewer, writing teacher and life-long student of writing. My experience as a teacher convinces me that it will help you regardless of the stage of your writing career, although it is directed towards non-professionals, particularly young students of writing.

The chapters follow the class-by-class content of my story writing courses. Each chapter, for the most part, analyzes a principle, cites examples from the writings of the masters of story-telling, refers to examples in the book's appendix and summarizes the main points.

I avoided the textbook approach and used the "I and you" style throughout. Famed educator Booker T. Washington said the ideal school is a log in the woods with a student on one end and a teacher on the other. That is the way I imagined it as I wrote this book, and my end was hard and bumpy. Hopefully you can imagine yourself on the other end, which, if I've done well, could be a bit softer and smoother.

To further bring the lessons "home," I have illustrated the points with anecdotes, both mine and those of other writers.

A unique aspect of this book is the appendix where excerpts from the writing of various authors and my analysis are designed to help you learn to apply analytical skill to YOUR reading. I am convinced that, in the end, one learns to write successfully by reading and writing, writing and reading.

As William Faulkner said: "Read, read, read. Read everything – trash, classics, good and bad, and see how they do it. Just like a carpenter who works as an apprentice and studies the master."

Have a happy read.

PART 1

The Approach

1 *The Miracle of the Blank Sheet of Paper*

Although I'm not a psychiatrist, I suspect everyone has a delicate ego. In any case, I know the writers I associate with, both the students and practitioners, have fragile egos. My ego is incredibly frail. I believe if you dragged out my ego and had a look, it would look like it hadn't slept for a week.

My brain tells me I can learn more from criticism than from praise, but my ego is hooked on praise.

I don't think my students can take criticism either. If that's true, how then does a writing teacher teach?

Very Interesting!

Perhaps I can use a photography analogy to explain.

I remember vividly the first photo I ever took and developed myself. The photo was simply a street scene in Chicago taken with my new Argus C3. Another resident of the YMCA hotel where I stayed told me (didn't show me) how to develop the film and make a print.

I followed directions as best I could, and in that dingy YMCA darkroom a miracle occurred when that white piece of photographic paper soaking in the developer began to show an image. Then came that glorious moment when I could actually recognize the street scene.

I took that picture to my room after it was dry and studied it. I put it away in a drawer; then took it out and admired it again. I tacked it up in a place where I could lay in bed and see it when I awoke.

I did not see that the picture was pale and washed out; that it was foggy and out of focus; that it was stained and scratched and covered with white blotches from dust on the negative.

Later, I took and developed many pictures. I studied photo magazines and checked out photo books from the library. By studying the masters, I learned to evaluate my work; to discard or make again pictures which didn't measure up. When I eventually left the YMCA hotel, that first print remained there . . . in the wastebasket.

As a photography teacher (as well as a writing teacher) I saw this wonder on the faces of my students again and again when their first picture began to take form in the developer. They would bring that pale, washed out, out-of-focus print to me, not saying anything, but waiting for my admiration. I would study it, turning it this way and that, and finally, giving it back, look the student in the eye, and say:

"Very interesting!"

It's not for me to criticize what you have put on that blank sheet of paper, whether it is a picture made with silver hallide crystals or a picture made with words. That's for you to do — to learn to do.

Teach you to write? I don't believe I can. I can, perhaps, teach you about writing and the best approach to learning the craft. I can, perhaps, help you learn to analyze the writing of others . . . the masters. And I can help you learn to apply this analysis to your own writing. Finally, I can, perhaps, help you get the courage to write, and — more importantly — to rewrite. As Ralph Waldo Emerson said: "Skill to do comes of doing."

Photographers photograph scenes, writers write scenes. If we writers do not develop a scene with clear, precise, vivid words it ends up pale and washed out. If we throw in commonplace, or obscure or vague words, the scene will become dark and murky. If we writers don't structure our stories the compositions end up confused and out of focus.

As with the photographer, we too start off with a blank sheet of paper and it is your job in reading this book to learn to fill it in until it is worth someone's time and money.

A Kink In Its Tail

Paul St. Pierre, the British Columbia author you may know best for his book *Breaking Smith's Quarter Horse*, wrote the following description in *Chilcotin Holiday* of a Chilcotin man he admired:

"All Lester's stories were masterpieces of the art of story-telling. Each was vivid. It was exciting. And there was a kink in the tail."

I would like you to engrave that description on your brain cells, or at least write it down in your notebook . . . that is story writing in a nutshell. And it is an outline for the organization of this book. First we study the techniques of vivid writing to get the reader involved; then we study the structure of a story to make it exciting. Finally, we study how to put a "kink in the tail" to make it memorable.

2 Why Write . . . When You Can Drive A Tractor?

A Member of Parliament invited to address the Ottawa Press Club started by saying: "We all learned to write in grade one, and some of us went on to better things."

I assume he was needling the assembled journalists in good spirits. But it is true. We all did learn to write in the first grade, and many people, not just MPs, believe that makes us all "writers."

One of my wives was a fiction writer. When we went to a cocktail party or other affair, we were usually introduced as "writers."

Inevitably during the course of the evening, someone – usually several someones – would come up to us and say:

"So, you're writers?"

We would nod in modest agreement.

Each of the questioners would continue with eyebrows raised, chin up and mouth pursed, and say aggressively:

"I've always intended to write, but I just haven't had time."

What an incredible insult!

They imply all it takes to be a writer is time. No skill, no talent, no training, no education, no apprenticeship, nothing to say . . . just time.

And they also imply writers have more time than other people. I don't know how that would be possible, but I wishtogawd it was true.

My brother, who is a photographer, reports he runs into the same attitude. Someone will admire one of his published photos by saying:

"Wow! What a great picture. What kind of camera do you have?"

To be a professional writer, all you need is time, and to be a professional photographer, all you need is a good camera.

So, if we all learned to write in the first grade, why are "writers" so rare? Try to find one in the Yellow Pages – pages jammed with doctors, lawyers, plumbers, dentists. Why not writers?

Perhaps I can explain. At the opening day of classes one year, a young man came up and told me why he was taking my writing class. "I was driving the tractor around and around the field plowing, and I thought: 'There must be an easier way to make a living.' So I decided to come here and become a writer."

He was back on the farm the day his first writing assignment was due. He had discovered writing for a reader was much, much harder than driving a tractor around and around.

The key phrase here is "writing for a reader." You are asking that a reader pay for your writing. That is much different from writing a letter to a friend, a memo to your boss or a report to your teacher – something like the difference between a family snapshot and a National Geographic cover.

As author/editor L. Rust Hills said: "The sinister thing about writing is that it starts off seeming so easy and ends up being so hard."

You learned to write in grade one. Now you should be prepared to learn to be a writer.

3 *Writers Write*

I put a piece of paper under my pillow, and
when I could not sleep, I wrote in the dark.
— Henry David Thoreau

Writers write. They don't think about it, dream about it or imagine it.

Writers write, and that truism could be the most difficult aspect of being a writer.

Writers write not knowing what the writing will to reveal about themselves. They can imagine a reader pointing a finger at the page with a gleeful look, saying: "Ha, ha, look at what this poor fool has written."

Writers write not knowing if anyone is ever going to read what is being written.

Writers write not knowing, each time they face the blank page, if they can write anything – that the page will not remain forever blank.

Writers write when they don't feel like writing.

I once received a five-page letter from Dorothy Johnson, author of *The Hanging Tree, The Man Who Shot Liberty Valance, A Man Called Horse* and others. She apologized for writing such a short letter, pointing out "my sciatica makes sitting at the typewriter excruciating."

There seems to be any number of reasons not to write. If you insist on writing anyway, here are some tricks.

One that works for me – gets me sitting down in front of the blank sheet of paper – is to define "work." I say to myself: Work is something you do when you would rather be doing something else. Right now, writing is what I would rather be doing.

The next trick is to actually put something down on that blank sheet of paper. This is the problem widely known as "writer's block."

At one point I was getting up at 5 a.m. and writing until leaving for my job as a reporter at 8 a.m. But suddenly, I couldn't put a thing down on paper. I would pour a cup of coffee; read over what I had written; pour another cup of coffee; read over what I had written . . . until it was time to go to my job. (Other writers report they endlessly sharpen pencils, even though they are using a typewriter.)

On that occasion I went to a hypnotist who convinced me it would be absolutely wonderful to finish the story I was working on. It worked. I couldn't wait to get to the typewriter the next morning, not even stopping to make a pot of coffee.

However, I have become convinced the cause of writer's block is the idea we get in our heads that what we write has to be perfect. Since then, whenever I have been stalled momentarily, I say to myself: Come on. Put something down, even if it's stupid!

I have found this trick much cheaper than going to a hypnotist.

Katherine Mansfield said: "Looking back, I imagine I was always writing. Twaddle it was too. But better to write twaddle or any-thing, anything, than nothing at all."

I hope you get the message. Do NOT put off writing until certain conditions are met – "I'll write when I'm not so busy." "I'll write when I get out of school." "I'll write when I get a cabin in the mountains."

My brother, when he was working on a book, rented a cabin in the Black Hills of South Dakota. He told me that after a month he started driving 30 miles into Rapid City every day so he could write on the computer in the city library among people.

Here's what Thoreau had to say about solitude:

I love to be alone. I never found the companion that was so companionable as solitude. We are for the most part more lonely when we go abroad among men than when we stay in our chambers. A man thinking or working is always alone, let him be where he will. Solitude is not measured by the miles of space that intervene between man and his fellows. The really diligent student in one of the crowded hives of Cambridge College is as solitary as a dervish in the desert.

Believe me, you don't have to WAIT until you're alone to write. You ARE alone. You write as you dream – alone.

4 How It's Done

> The best time for planning a book is
> while you're washing the dishes.
> — Agatha Christie

Many of my students have expressed a curiosity about how writers write – the actual act of writing. I find it interesting myself.

Carl Sandburg wrote every day from midnight to six a.m. He said he loved the quiet during those hours.

I have done the bulk of my writing in the midst of a chaotic newsroom – compressed air tubes overhead sucking copy in a clattering whoosh to the composing room; giggling reporters; mad dashes by late newspeople on deadline; shouts and sometimes cursing.

However, for freelance writing I always get up at 4 or 5 a.m. For one thing, there is absolutely nothing else to do at that time of morning (if you are out of bed). One must write.

Agatha Christie, one of the most prolific authors in history, had a daughter, Rosalind, who said she never knew her mother was a writer until she was a teenager and one of her teachers mentioned it.

Christie wrote whenever she had a spare ten or fifteen minutes. She never made a fuss about it. She never said: "Now be quiet. Your mommy is going to write."

An interviewer once asked to take her picture in her writing room. But she had no such thing. She said she sometimes wrote on the marble top table in her bedroom which held the wash basin; on the dining room table between meals, or anywhere there was a flat place handy when she had a few spare minutes.

On several occasions when I have been busy on other things, I have used her method. It worked. I managed to produce a fair amount in ten- or fifteen-minute sessions.

For the most part, however, as a freelancer I have a ritualistic early morning schedule and write for about four hours, producing about four pages.

But there are wide variations. Louis L'Amour put out five pages a day. Others as few as one.

Four hours may seem like a short work day, but writing requires total concentration and involvement. You may be as exhausted after four hours of writing as you would be after eight hours of digging post holes.

Making it a ritual seems to work for many writers. I have found it something of a chore to get started on a new project, but in a few days it has developed into a comfortable routine.

But there are many ways. I have two friends who, with their portable computers, write together – each on her own book. They write all day and into the night, producing several chapters in their marathon. And then they might not write again for a week.

5 *The Summing Up*

I was camping with the family one summer on Vancouver Island when a man in the adjoining campsite came over.

I invited him to coffee, and as we were getting acquainted, he said he was a high school principal. I said I was a writer.

"Oh," he said, with a tiny, pretentious smile curling the edges of his mouth, "I've always intended to do some writing, but I just haven't had time."

Something snapped. I leaped to my feet.

"You know," I said, gritting my teeth, "I've always intended to do some high school principaling, but I haven't had time until now."

He stood up and started moving away. I followed him.

"It wouldn't require any education would it? No practice? No study? No apprenticeship?"

By this time he was moving down the path towards his camp, looking fearfully over his shoulder.

I cupped my hands around my mouth and shouted after him: "I HAVE THE TIME! I HAVE THE TIME!"

It's Your Turn

When you next go to your writing desk or the kitchen table, I want you to relax for a moment and say to yourself: *Right now, I would rather be doing this than anything else.*

And when you face that blank page or that blank computer screen, I want you to grit your teeth and say to yourself: *I'm going to put something down even if it's stupid.*

And finally, I want you to imagine cupping your hands around your mouth and shouting: *I have the time! I have the time!*

Precisely the same amount of time as has everyone.

What They Say

Writing is a dog's life, but the only life worth living.

— Gustave Flaubert

The tools I need for my work are paper, tobacco, food, and a little whisky.

— William Faulkner

It is a fact that few novelists enjoy the creative labour, though most enjoy thinking about the creative labour.

— Arnold Bennett

What release to write so that one forgets oneself, forgets one's companion, forgets where one is or what one is going to do next – to be drenched in sleep or in the sea. Pencils and pads and curling blue sheets alive with letters heap up on the desk.

— Anne Morrow Lindbergh

. . . What a QUEER business writing is! I don't know, I don't believe other people are ever as foolishly excited as I am while I'm working. I've BEEN this man, BEEN this woman. I've stood for hours on the Auckland wharf. I've been out in the stream waiting to be berthed – I've been a seagull hovering at the stern and a hotel porter whistling through his teeth. It isn't as though one sits and watches the spectacle. That would be thrilling enough, God knows. But one IS the spectacle for the time. If one remained oneself all the time it would be a bit less exhausting.

— Katherine Mansfield in a letter to a friend after finishing *The Stranger*, a New Zealand story.

PART II

The Presentation

6   *A Long Patience*

You should be cautious when you come across how-to-write articles or books titled "The Secret of . . . "

There are no secrets to writing, and if there were, we writers probably wouldn't tell anyone. Who needs competition? And in any case, an article titled: "The Secret of . . ." is a contradiction in terms because it would not be a secret if revealed in the article.

Nevertheless, IF there were a secret, that secret would be "scene writing."

Some stories are written as a single scene, as in a short story or a one-act play; or as a series of scenes, as in a novel or a full-length stage or screen drama. There are exceptions. Some short stories have more than one scene, and some three-act plays, such as *The Four Poster*, have only one scene.

Scenes are written by most authors so smoothly and with such subtle transitions from one scene to the next, we readers are not aware that what we are reading are scenes. But for you writing students it is necessary to turn on your analytic powers when you read, and to be aware.

A scene comprises only three elements: description of setting, description of action and dialogue. Beginning writers also include "explanation" by interjecting themselves and telling readers what the characters are thinking, or explaining what is happening. But this is rarely effective.

Readers do not want to be TOLD. They want to FIND OUT and to find out through what is happening and what is being said.

Reading is an adventure. We readers do not know what is going to happen next, how it is going to happen or to whom it is going to happen. We read to find out, not to be told.

For you, as the writer, to stop the story and explain to readers what is happening, rather than allowing them to discover it, would be as awful as interrupting with the punch line as someone is telling a joke. Or, have you ever heard anything so pathetic as someone explaining a joke?

Anton Chekhov wrote that most beginners should take their story, "fold it in half and tear up the first part." He indicated that they usually spend the first half explaining what the story is going to be about, rather than "getting right into it." He adds: "One must write so that the reader should understand, without the author's explanations, what it is all about."

Sean O'Faolain, in his fine book *The Short Story*, explains that "telling never dilates the mind as implication does." He goes on to point out what we readers find out from the opening sentence of Chekhov's story, *The Lady With the Dog*. The sentence: "It was reported that a new face had been seen on the quay; a lady with a little dog."

O'Faolain explains:

We gather, altogether by implication, that the scene is laid in a port. We gather that this port is a seaside resort, for ladies with dogs do not perambulate on commercial docks. We gather that the season is fine weather – probably summer or autumn. We gather that this seaside resort is a sleepy, unfrequented little place for one does not observe new faces at big, crowded places. Furthermore, the phrase "it was reported" implies that gossip circulates in a friendly way at this sleepy resort.

We can imagine how much time it would take and how boring it would be to have all that told at length.

Another example of imagination "dilating the mind" is the fact that popular radio dramas rarely survived translation into television or the movies. *The Shadow Knows* simply lost all its spookiness when viewers could see the Shadow in action, rather than having to imagine him.

The art of story writing is the art of withholding information. One should think of a story as the UNFOLDING of events like a Japanese paper flower in a tumbler of water.

At this point, I can understand a student's impatience. "I thought this was a writing book. I want to write!"

I shrug and say: "Go ahead. No one is stopping you."

I have had some adult students who have made a career of taking writing courses. Their theory is, apparently, that when they have learned everything there is to know about writing . . . then they will write.

In the meantime, a book such as this must analyze by TEARING DOWN and examining the parts, while writing is creative, PUTTING TOGETHER and filling a blank page. Hopefully, filling it with something wonderful.

There seems to be a conflict here, but the human mind is a wonderful instrument. It can both LEARN by tearing apart, and CREATE by putting together, in its own way, what it has learned. As I said in Chapter 1, I can't teach you to write, but I can help you learn about writing.

Guy de Maupassant wrote:

. . . At a later date, Flaubert, whom I had occasionally met, took a fancy to me. I ventured to show him a few attempts. He read them kindly and replied: "I cannot tell whether you will have any talent. What you have brought me proves a certain intelligence, but never forget this, young man: Talent is nothing but long patience. Go and work."

7 *Getting the Reader Involved*

As I have pointed out, stories are written in scenes whether those stories are presented as a movie, television drama or stage play; in a novel, short story or memoir.

A movie may have hundreds of scenes; a play usually fewer than a dozen. My novel had 36 scenes, and most short stories have only one. There are exceptions.

The play *The Four Poster* has only two characters, and one scene. It all takes place on or around a four-poster bed (and three characters would be a crowd.)

As mentioned, a scene is simple, containing only three elements – setting, action and dialogue.

However, most beginning writers try to add a fourth – explanation. They assume the reader can't understand, and decide to interject themselves into the story to explain the characters' thoughts. In other words, to "tell," not "show" the reader.

One of the advantages of a novel or short story is that a writer CAN describe thoughts, while it is nearly impossible in a movie or stage play. But today's reader will not sit still for it, except in small doses.

The fundamental goal in writing a scene is to get the reader involved. When the writer stops the action and takes the reader into the character's mind in order to explain, it breaks this magic connection.

In "real life" we *discover* what is going on by observing and listening, and readers also want to *discover* what's going on in the story in much the same manner.

Stick with describing action and setting, and reporting dialogue.

In light of the above, it is fitting, therefore, that the first step in learning writing techniques should be to look at "description."

The only purpose of description is to get the reader involved. To get the reader to BE THERE, and to become part of the action and the setting. If the heroine cries, we want the reader to cry; if the back of the hero's neck tingles as he enters the darkened house, we want the reader's neck to tingle.

We don't use description to knock the reader's eyes out, or to impress the reader with our beautiful writing. Samuel Johnson said: "Read over your compositions and, when you meet a passage which you think is particularly fine, strike it out."

Affective description – the kind that will engage the emotions of your reader – has three main aspects.

(I will use the term "metaphor" here in the broad sense to include such figures of speech as simile and personification.)

Metaphor – Saying another thing about a thing. (Larkish little children . . . brows like fingernails)

Strong verbs – Use adjectives sparingly, and avoid the "to be" verbs (was, is, were, there are, etc.)

Details, details, details – The "little particulars" of seeing, smelling, tasting, feeling, hearing – (involve all of the reader's senses.)

Now that seems simple enough. And the concepts are simple.

One other aspect of description – RARELY stop the story to describe the setting. Incorporate setting into the action.

For inspiration in writing your descriptive scene you should examine in the Appendix *The Turtle* by John Steinbeck, the first paragraphs of *Grizzly Country* by Andy Russell and the little piece at the end of the Appendix which I wrote.

If you feel you have to describe a sunset, put it in a footnote.

– Jack Woodford

8   *Made Bold by Rum and Desperation*

The following is James Houston's description of Shoona, an Inuit shaman, who is lying sick in the igloo of the narrator of the book *Spirit Wrestler*.

> *Even in his weakened condition, Shoona was a masterly storyteller, made bold perhaps by the effect of rum and desperation. He did not hesitate to imitate the voices or the songs of other people, the sounds of animals, or even the whistling wind and driving snow. He used any device to give his story a sense of life. He spoke simply, using common words, making sure I would understand . . .*

This is your job. In making sure the reader understands, use any device to give your story a sense of life. Imitate the voices and the sounds and use common language (but not commonplaces). Do not be afraid. Open up (made bold, perhaps, by desperation.) Become a master storyteller.

Writing is the Long Patience

A writer's fantasy is sitting at the keyboard and, in the throes of ecstasy, the words flow effortlessly onto the blank page. The reality is that a writer sits on a chair, beads of sweat on the forehead. The writer squirms, looks out the window; then Xs out or hits the delete button wiping out what was written and starts again.

In the end, there is a written page, or two or three or four. And those pages will have to be rewritten – probably several times.

The reason for all this is that if you write the first thing that comes into your mind, it will almost always be a cliché or a commonplace – not the kind of writing that will get the reader involved.

I have already referred to Chekhov. He is considered by many to be the father of the modern short story. He also wrote vividly about the craft. In a letter he wrote:

In my opinion a true description of nature should be very brief and have a character of relevance. Commonplaces such as: 'The setting sun bathing in the waves of the darkening sea, poured its purple, gold, etc. . . the swallows flying over the surface of the water twittered merrily . . .' such commonplaces one ought to abandon. In descriptions of nature one ought to seize upon the little particulars, grouping them in such a way that, when you shut your eyes, you get the picture, For instance, you will get the full effect of a moonlight night if you write that on the mill-dam a little glowing star-point flashed from the neck of a broken bottle, and the round, black shadow of a wolf emerged . . .

Details are the thing. God preserve us from commonplaces.

One often gets these "little particulars" and the precise metaphor (one which doesn't stop the story but adds to the vividness of the image) during the chore of re-writing, re-writing, re-writing.

You will find many examples of what Chekhov had to say in the works of the masters which are excerpted in the Appendix of this book, particularly Steinbeck's *The Turtle*.

The Interminable Transition

A scene has two main purposes: To move the story along, and to reveal the character – often both. In rare situations, it can also be used to set the stage, as in Steinbeck's *The Turtle*, a transitional chapter in *The Grapes of Wrath*. (The chapter doesn't have a title, but numerous anthologies which reprinted this chapter titled it *The Turtle*.)

If your scene does none of these things, whack it out!

One problem many writers have is in handling transitions between scenes – getting their characters from one place to another.

The most commonly used transition between scenes is a blank line. The best known transition is "Meanwhile, back at the ranch . . ."

It is easy to fall into the trap of writing "the interminable transition," described by William Knott in *The Craft of Fiction*. If you have your character leave one scene, open the door, go down the hallway, down the stairs, get into a taxicab, ride through city streets, one block, two blocks three . . . open the door; get out of the taxicab, cross the sidewalk, open the door . . . you have written the interminable transition.

Your character will get to the next scene, but your reader will not. Use a blank line, and then write: "Arriving at the office of her publisher, she . . ."

What They Say

A good style should show no sign of effort. What is written should seem a happy accident. I think no one in France now writes more admirably than Colette, and such is the ease of her expression that you cannot bring yourself to believe that she takes any trouble over it. I asked her. I was exceedingly surprised to hear that she wrote everything over and over again. She told me that she would often spend a whole morning upon a single page. But it does not matter how one gets the effect of ease. For my part, if I get it at all, it is only by strenuous effort. Nature seldom provides me with the word, the turn of phrase, that is appropriate without being far-fetched or commonplace.

– W. Somerset Maugham

I have rewritten – often several times – every word I have ever published. My pencils outlast their erasers.

– Vladimir Nabokov

9 *"Help!" He Said Helplessly*

"He said" (or "she said") should be the most common phrase in your story – by far the most common phrase. If it's not, you had better take a look at the story and see if you are "telling" it rather than "showing" it.

In "real life" we get to know the people in our circle of acquaintance by what they say and what they do. In other words, dialogue and action. It usually takes a long time to get to know someone well because we are only rarely invited inside someone's head and allowed to know what they are thinking.

Exactly the same is true in story writing. You should only rarely allow the reader to get inside the head of one of your characters. While you, of course, know what the character is thinking, the reader, for the most part, wants to "discover" through action and dialogue, and not be "told."

Readers will not know completely the main character until the end of the story, nor do they want to. So, relax. Let dialogue and action reveal the characters bit by bit, exactly the same as happens in "real life."

This is not to say, however, that dialogue should drift aimlessly; that the characters should endlessly talk small talk as in "real life." Remember Hayakawa's definition: "Abstracting only the significant events and organizing them into a meaningful significance constitutes the storyteller's art."

Keep firmly in mind that the dialogue should reveal character and move the story along. If it doesn't do either of these things, slash it out.

Be careful you do not use dialogue to EXPLAIN. Your characters must talk to each other – not to the reader.

An example of talking to the reader:

The phone rang, and she answered: "Why, hello John, the wastrel son of the richest man in town. How are you?"

The only thing worse would be to have her thinking:

The phone rang and she thought: That is probably John, the wastrel son of the richest man in town.

You could write it this way:

Picking up the phone, Jane answered: "John? . . . you're slurring your words . . . No, I don't know what you did after you left the country club dance . . . Well, don't worry, if you got in trouble your Dad will buy you out of it."

Here, we are learning much about John by what she said, and by what our imagination tells us he said – all through a few lines of well-chosen dialogue. We also learn that Jane is a plain-spoken Jane without much sympathy for John's problems, and we get a suggestion of the problem that will face them in this story.

We writers have to work hard at having our characters appear to speak naturally. We do not want the reader to catch on that we are selecting the conversation for a purpose. The dialogue we write is not "natural" conversation, but must carry the illusion of natural conversation. It's tricky.

I will have some tips for you in handling the mechanics of dialogue, but you must read and analyze the dialogue as written by the masters. And you must write.

As to using that four-letter word "said," its job is to leave the reader with absolutely no confusion over who is talking, yet be so unobtrusive that the reader is not aware it is there. Tricky? You bet.

Following are some how-to and how-not-to ways of using "said."

From St. Pierre's *Breaking Smith's Quarter Horse*, this is the way the master did it:

"Are you all right?" she said.

He kept walking towards her. "I do not get mad very often," he said.

"Don't get mad, Smith."

"I do not get mad very often, I said – "

"Smith, don't lose your temper."

" – but when I say to leave that bloody gun on the bloody wall that is what I bloody well mean."

When only two people are in the scene, and when one says something, and the other clearly responds, there is no need for "he said" or "she said" except in lengthy dialogue where one is needed occasionally to make sure the reader doesn't get confused.

Another way to avoid too many "saids" is to have the person use the other's name: "Smith, don't lose your temper" is obviously said by her. (Normally, a wife would not use her husband's last name, but in this case it has already been made clear this is the way she talks to him.)

Another (wrong) way of using "said."

She said: "Are you all right?"

He said: "I do not get mad very often."

She said: "Don't get mad, Smith."

He said: "I do not get mad very often, I said – "

She said: "Smith don't lose your temper."

Another wrong way is putting it in the present tense:

"Are you all right?" she says.

"I do not get mad very often," he says.

"Don't get mad, Smith," she says.

Playing a game with "said" and using substitutes was a style used by the Nancy Drew stories in which characters exclaimed, contradicted, declared, concurred . . .

"Are you all right?" she questioned.

"I do not get mad very often," he claimed.

"Don't get mad, Smith," she pleaded.

Another ploy in a boys book series, Tom Swift, used adverbs telling "how" it was said:

"Are you all right," she said fearfully.

"I do not get mad very often," he said sternly.

"Don't get mad, Smith," she said beseechingly.

There is a party game where the guests make up "Tom Swifties," such as: "Pass the pineapple," he said dolefully. Or, "My roommate moved out," he said fruitlessly. Or, "The oil spill wasn't my fault," he said exoneratedly.

One can mix action with dialogue, but it must be done judiciously. The wrong way:

She took a step back, her hand rising involuntarily to her lower lip, "Are you all right?"

He kept walking towards her. "I do not get mad very often."

"Don't get mad, Smith." Her eyes would not meet his.

All of the above "bad" examples can be used effectively when they are used judiciously. St. Pierre uses the adverbial way only once in this chapter-long scene of dialogue, but it is perfect. Here it is:

(Smith has discovered that the murderer, Gabriel, plans to have Smith turn him in and collect the reward money – using the money for Gabriel's defense in court.)

"Now," said Smith, "be reasonable, man. How could I possibly manage that?"

"Ain't very hart, I ton't think," said Gabriel softly.

Because it hasn't been used before, the "said softly" takes on significance. We readers feel its hint of danger.

St. Pierre uses action throughout this scene to break up the long passages of dialogue. However, it is used in appropriate places that contribute to our involvement, not scattered indiscriminately interfering with dialogue.

Gabriel said, "I get scared cause there is only one door this place."

"I know exactly what you mean," said Smith, "but it would be more sensible if you came up and smoked a cigarette and we will talk some. I will twist one for each of us." He started again, blowing a leaf of paper loose at the top of the Chanticleer packet with a light puff of his breath. After he had gently pulled the paper free he turned for the first time, to look at the corner beside the door. "Come on, friend," he said, "let's light up a smoke."

(Note also, the details, the "little particulars," in the description of the action that put us readers THERE.)

When a conversation is broken up this way by action, what is said following the action takes on greater importance. This is what is called "the pregnant pause" in play writing.

Here is an example from Beryl Markham's *West With the Night* at the end of the chapter "Errands of the Wind."

"Ruta," I said, "I think I am going to leave all this and learn to fly."

He stood in a loose-box beside a freshly groomed colt – a young colt gleaming like light on water. There was a body-brush in

Ruta's hand, its bristles intertwined with hairs from the colt. Ruta removed the hairs with slow fingers and hung the brush on a peg. He looked out the stable door into the near distance where Menegai shouldered a weightless cloud. He shrugged and dusted dustless hands, one against the other.

He said, "If it is to be that we must fly, Memsahib, then we will fly. At what hour of the morning do we begin?"

Whew! That's almost a nine-month pregnant pause between what she said, and what he answered. But what Ruta had to say certainly doesn't get lost in the middle of the dialogue. And this is, after all, a major turning point in the life of Beryl Markham.

Note again the details – the "little particulars" – in the description of the action, and the metaphor – the shouldered cloud (personification) that puts us readers there.

The four most common errors my students commit when they first begin writing dialogue are:

Having all the characters talk like English professors, rather than each character talk in an individual way. Not even English professors talk like English professors.

Having the characters make speeches every time they open their mouths, rather than in short, often incomplete and ungrammatical sentences.

Having the characters talk to the reader, rather than to each other.

Having "he (or she) said" used awkwardly, bringing it to the conscious attention of the reader.

What They Say

The situation of my tale, and its descriptive and narrative portions, I am conscious of conducting, though often unaware of how the story first came to me, pleading to be told; but when the dialogue begins, then I become merely a recording instrument, and my hand never hesitates because my mind has not to choose, but only to set down what these stupid or intelligent, lethargic or passionate, people say to each other in a language, and with arguments that appear to be all their own. . . . The vital dialogue is that exchanged by characters who their creator has really vitalized, and only the significant passages of their talk should be recorded . . .

— Edith Wharton in *Confessions of a Novelist*

PART III

The Elements

10 *The Elements of a Story*

E. M. Forster, author of *A Passage to India* and other books widely known in English literature, gave a series of lectures on writing which were collected into a book titled *Aspects of the Novel* first published in 1927. It is considered by many to be the definitive work on fiction writing.

Here are the opening two paragraphs:

THE STORY – We shall all agree that the fundamental aspect of the novel is its storytelling aspect, but we shall voice our assent in different tones, and it is on the precise tone of voice we employ now that our subsequent conclusions will depend.

Let us listen to three voices. If you ask one type of man, 'What does a novel do?' he will reply placidly: 'Well – I don't know – it seems a funny sort of question to ask – a novel's a novel – well, I don't know – I suppose it kind of tells a story, so to speak.' He is quite good tempered and vague, and probably driving a motorbus at the same time and paying no more attention to literature than it merits. Another man whom I visualize as on a golf course, will be aggressive and brisk. He will reply: 'What does a novel do? Why, tell a story of course, and I've no use for it if it didn't. I like a story. You can take your art, you can take your literature, you can take your music, but give me a good story. And I like a story to be a story, mind, and my wife's the same.' And a third man, he says in a sort of drooping regretful voice, 'Yes – oh dear yes – the novel tells a story.' I respect and admire the first speaker. I detest and fear the second. And the third is myself. Yes – oh dear yes – the novel tells a story. That is the fundamental aspect without which it could not exist. That is the highest factor common to all novels, and I wish that it was not so, that it could be something different – melody, or perception of the truth, not this low atavistic form.

Oh dear yes, I'm afraid you are going to have to learn to tell a story. And fortunately, the elements of a story and its structure are well known. They have had at least since the time of Neanderthal Man to be developed, hence Forster's reference to "atavistic form." The shape of the Neanderthal skull cavity indicates an ability to talk. And if there was talk there were certainly stories.

Forster's music analogy can be pursued on two lines of thought. As writers, we can imagine ourselves as the director of a great orchestra gripped by inspiration as the music washes over us. But it would be more realistic to imagine ourselves as the flautist in the orchestra struggling with the notes, and who has spent years learning the craft. Or even closer to ourselves, the writer of the music struggling with point and counterpoint; harmony, time, key, etc.

That idea need not be discouraging. After all, a flautist while learning the craft is enjoying music, as are the director and composer, and while you are learning your craft, you can be enjoying stories. In fact, you are probably never going to stop learning. I know that the second half of my novel is better written because of what I learned writing the first half.

Another thought is that while music appears to be formless, it in fact follows a rigid, almost mathematical form. Some writing students seem to feel that learning the structure and form of storytelling is beneath them – that somehow, the form is going to limit their creativity. That to be "original" they must invent a new way to tell a story. That to follow the traditional "form" is to write "formula writing."

When we listen to Beethoven we become involved. Beethoven's first four notes – ta-ta-ta dum – in the Fifth Symphony get us every time and from then on we don't notice that he is using only endless variations of one theme; that he is using only an eight-note scale; that a symphony has four parts; that it has a theme which ties it all together. Beethoven did not create the eight note scale. He did not create the four part structure of a symphony. He did not come up with the idea of theme. Does this mean, then, that Beethoven was not creative? Was he nothing but a "formula music writer?"

As concertgoers, we do not notice the structure as we get caught up in the symphony, and as readers, we do not notice the structure as we get caught up in the story.

Oh dear yes, I wish that writing was like listening to music, not this low, atavistic struggle with structure – not this mental anguish of getting the words right, of stopping when we reach the end and of starting at the ta-ta-ta dum.

This is the way Paul St. Pierre put it in the preface to his literary classic *Breaking Smith's Quarter Horse*:

If there is a moral in this book, it is not my fault. If there is social relevance, it crept in without alerting me, in which case I would have hit it with a stick. This is a story, nothing more. I make no apologies for calling it a story. In my view, the only reason for writing a book is to tell a story.

So. Here we are. What is a story, then?

If we imagine the story as a skeleton, the backbone would be TIME – this happens, then this happens, then this happens . . . then . . .

There have been attempts to avoid or obscure time – books by Gertrude Stein, and James Joyce's *Ulysses*, for example.

But accepting time as the story's backbone, the job of an author is clear – to make the reader want to know what happens next. If you fail as a writer, it will because you did not make the reader want to know what happens next.

As Forster pointed out in his lectures, you must think of yourself as Scheherazade who had learned her husband wanted to secretly kill her at night, but he couldn't because she told him stories all night (for 1001 nights), and always left him in the morning in the middle of a story wanting to know what was going to happen next – "At this moment Scheherazade saw the morning appearing and, discreet, was silent."

One could also imagine that storytelling Neanderthal Man, failing to keep his campfire companions wanting to know what happened next, would be set upon with clubs.

Forster points out that even though the writing may be bad, a story can still be a success . . . if a reader wants to know what happens next. He describes Sir Walter Scott as a very bad writer, but a success because he knew how to tell a story.

To make his point, Forster quotes Scott in *The Antiquary* at a point in the story when the main characters, Sir Arthur and Isabella, are cut off by a rising tide while walking along the ocean.

While they exchanged these words they paused upon the highest ledge of rock to which they could attain; for it seemed that any farther attempt to move forward could only serve to anticipate their fate. Here then they were to await the sure, though slow progress of the raging element, something in the situation of the martyrs of the Early Church, who, exposed by heathen tyrants to be slain by wild beasts, were compelled for a time to witness the impatience and rage by which the animals were agitated, while awaiting the signal for undoing their grates and letting them loose upon the victims.

Yet even this fearful pause gave Isabella time to collect the powers of a mind naturally strong and courageous, and which rallied itself at this terrible juncture. 'Must we yield life,' she said, 'without a struggle? Is there no path, however dreadful, by which we could climb the crag, or at least attain some height above the tide, where we could remain till morning, or till help comes? They must be aware of our situation, and will raise the country to relieve us.'

When you stop laughing at this incredibly artificial dialogue, the awkward "she said," and the long-winded metaphor, wouldn't you still like to know what happens next?

So. There you have it. If the fundamental aspect of the novel is its storytelling aspect, then the fundamental aspect of the story is "what's going to happen next." And since, as Forster points out, this depends on time – the story has to have a clear time frame.

All the techniques we will be talking about, therefore, will be within the framework of making the reader want to know what happens next. To fail will be as fatal to you as a writer as it would have been to Scheherazade – although not as permanent. If you fail, you can try again.

The Elements

SUSPENSE – The first element is "suspense." How do you attain it? One of the ways is, again, time – the lack of it. I wonder how writers managed suspense before the invention of the time bomb? I don't know how many adventure stories I have read which depended on a time bomb for their suspense. *The Guns of Navarrone* is one that comes quickly to mind. Nothing seems to develop suspense better than having your characters have to get someplace or do something by a certain time, and (drumbeat) TIME IS RUNNING OUT. Just try to put a story down at that point.

Suspense is also developed by foreshadowing. Depending on who you are writing for, you can beat the reader over the head with foreshadowing: "Little did she know that when next she saw Tara it would be a heap of ashes," or you can be beautifully subtle about it such as in stories by John Steinbeck.

I recommend you study the opening scene of Steinbeck's *Of Mice and Men* where big ol' lummox Lennie is caught with a dead mouse in his pocket and he protests that he only wanted to pet it. We readers suspect that Lennie pets things until they die . . . and we read on.

CHARACTER – We readers must CARE what happens next, and caring involves people. Even if our characters are animals, they have people characteristics. Characters are probably the most fascinating and memorable aspect of a story. Hear the words *Gone with the Wind* and the first thing that comes into your mind is Scarlett O'Hara or, perhaps, Rhett Butler.

To be memorable, the main characters, even the villains, must be strong, aggressive types who take charge of their own lives, and often the lives of the people around them. We could go on and on about characters in stories – and we will in future lessons. How about Scrooge and Tiny Tim in *A Christmas Carol*, or Rosie and Charlie in *The African Queen*?

CONFLICT – If there is no conflict, nothing is going to happen next. . . and the reader will know it. If you were Scheherazade, you wouldn't see the next sunrise.

Conflict is simple. It's merely character vs. character; character vs. themselves; character vs. nature. You must have one of these conflicts in your story, and in most cases, all three.

For example, in *The African Queen,* C. S. Forester has Rosie, a very proper spinster missionary, trapped on a small boat on a river in the African jungle in the middle of a war, with Charlie, a gin-drinking, shiftless Cockney boat captain.

Clearly, Forester is going to have some character vs. character conflict between Rosie and Charlie!

And there is going to be some character vs. themselves conflict as Rosie and Charlie each struggle with their backgrounds in this close-knit, romantic situation.

When the two decide to take the boat down an unnavigable river to sink a German warship, we readers know we are going to be exposed to some character vs. nature conflict – the people vs. the river. So . . . what's going to happen next? Read on . . .

CHANGE – Another essential element of a story is change. The characters, the circumstances, the lives, maybe even the world, must not be the same at the end of the story. Often children, when writing stories, have their hero involved in an incredible adventure . . . and then wake up from a dream. When you read such a story you groan. And if you read the story to a group, there would be a collective groan because "NOTHING HAPPENED!" When we say "nothing happened" in a story we mean there has been no change.

The boy who wakes up is the same boy who went to bed and became involved in the incredible adventure.

One of my students wanted me to read a short story she had written but had been unable to sell. She said it was a good story because "it really happened," not realizing that real happenings hardly ever make a story, although they often form the basis for a story.

Her story involved a secretary who, after partying all night and feeling frail, left work early the next day to go home.

At her apartment she went immediately to bed after setting her alarm for the usual 7 a.m. the next morning. When the alarm went off, she felt like she had hardly been to bed, but she dutifully got up and looked out the window into the dim light of dawn. She then fixed her usual toast and eggs, dressed, and left for work.

On stepping out of the house she discovered it was pitch dark.

You see, you can't set the alarm on a non-digital clock for 7 a.m. the NEXT DAY. So, at 7 p.m. that same day, what she thought was the dim light of sunrise was actually the dim light of sunset.

That's a cute anecdote. But it's not a story. If you had invested your time in reading it, you would have felt cheated, because "NOTHING HAPPENED."

As a reader you would know the secretary went back to bed and got up the next morning the same humdrum girl and went off to her same humdrum life.

I recall a short short story published on one page in Colliers magazine just after the Second World War. This was a period of time when Allied occupation troops were not allowed to "fraternize with the enemy." That is, the "female" enemy. In fact, they could fraternize all they wanted (and did), but what they couldn't do was marry the German girls, under the theory, I guess, that the Army had to save the lonesome boys for their hometown girls.

This story opens on a dark street in Berlin, with only a single light showing through a store front window down the street. A young man in a civilian suit is striding down the sidewalk when a girl steps out of a dark doorway, falls into step with him, and says in a fake, sexy voice:

"How about coming up to see me? Only 10 Marks."

He continues to stride down the street and explains:

"No, thanks. I've just got off the plane from New York City and I can't wait to see my girl, Yolanda. I know she didn't believe me when I said I was going to go back to the States, get my discharge from the Army and return to marry her. I can't wait to see her face when she sees me."

Just then, they pass in front of the lighted store window. The young man looks at the girl, stops and says in a pained, strangled voice:

"Yolanda!"

Well, that's a story. It has suspense, characters, conflict and CHANGE. We readers know that the lives of these two characters have changed dramatically and irrevocably. Their relationship will never be the same again.

INCREDIBLE – A story must be incredible. Incredible in the same way that gossip is incredible. One does not bother to relate and pass on ordinary events. We ask breathlessly:

"Did you hear . . ."

Then we proceed to tell about some unusual event – the more incredible the better. When I teach journalism, I define "news" as whatever makes people say: *"Wow!"* And that, for the most part, is also what a story is.

Some authors take an apparently ordinary event such as Carson McCullers' *The Member of the Wedding*, and make it extraordinary as seen through the eyes of an unique character: "Frankie, a freakishly tall girl stumbling awkwardly and shyly into adolescence . . ." according to the editor's preface. One can also imagine in this small southern town the gossip – "Did you hear . . . Frankie wanted to go on the honeymoon with her sister and her new husband!"

One of Steinbeck's great works is *The Pearl*. It's about the poorest man in the world finding the largest pearl in the world. Incredible? Of course. We do not want to read about an *ordinary* man finding an *ordinary* pearl because it's not the sort of event that would cause us to say, breathlessly:

"Did you hear . . ."

11 *The Dramatic Form*

We probably all agree that in telling a joke one should put the punch line at the end. Surprisingly, there are those who would argue a story does not have a structure. That to follow a form would not be creative.

I have had a number of students who were going to set the literary world on its ear, and invent a new story structure. In fact, there are markets for such experimental works – the "little" literary magazines which pay with a free copy of the magazine. Most of their stories are actually "vignettes" or incidents. They lack the "meaningful significance" of Hayakawa's story definition, and at least some are written by writers without the skill to tell a real story. Do not confuse the terms "literary" and "literature."

A U.S. national magazine, under a new editor, tried this route. The typical "story" would have someone (an unnamed, undescribed someone) go for a walk and think about life. As I write this, the magazine has a new editor, is publishing real stories and engaging in a massive advertising campaign to lure back all the readers it lost.

The form now followed by the magazine to recapture its readers is called *"The Dramatic Form."*

This form probably dates back to Neanderthal Man (perhaps even further); continues through the Bible stories; through Louis L'Amour and John Steinbeck, and no doubt will continue forever.

It's the form that makes sense out of life; we apparently desperately need form, for when we had evolved to the point where we could anticipate our deaths, we needed something to cling to when all rational evidence indicated life was meaningless. This is why "real life" does not make a story. Consider what happens at the end in real life? If you were going to write the actual day-to-day "life" of Charles Lindbergh, 50 percent of your story would take place during the time he lived in Hawaii as a recluse – the last 10 percent spent dying of cancer.

Readers, therefore, demand the story structure be followed. It's our way of believing that life makes sense. It is a form that works in telling a story in the same way that putting the punch line at the end works in telling a joke. It is what Forster calls "the chopped-off length of the tapeworm of time."

The form is simple to write down, but perhaps, not as simple to apply. It is: Beginning, middle, climax, denouement and end. That is, a story is divided into five parts, and all are usually necessary. Occasionally, a short-short story may begin with the denouement; skipping a beginning and an ending. But it would not be wise to be concerned with exceptions until you have learned to handle the rule.

One of the ways to help in understanding the Dramatic Form is to visualize it. This can be done by putting it into a graph.

In the following graph, the horizontal line measures the story in "time." The vertical scale measures the story in emotional "intensity."

The Dramatic Form

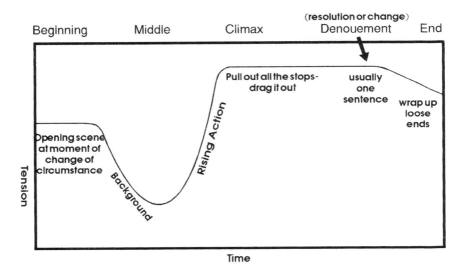

THE BEGINNING – Starts at a point of relatively high tension, usually at the moment of a change in circumstance for the main character or characters (in some writing books designated as the protagonists) such as arriving somewhere, or leaving, or someone else arriving or leaving.

A caution: Do not start at too high a point in the story. Louis L'Amour wrote that he once started a story about a prize fighter with an incredibly vivid prize fight scene, but was forced to abandon the story because there was no place to go from there except downhill.

THE MIDDLE – From the opening, the story goes down in intensity and is usually involved in disclosing background, such as the reason for the characters being in a moment of change. This is usually done through action and dialogue. (Although "flashback" can be used, this tends to stop the story – to explain – and should only rarely be attempted. Scheherazade would never have tried it.)

As the story continues, the conflicts you have set in motion begin to intensify and the reader becomes more and more involved with the situation and the characters. Readers cannot be kept on the edge of their seats constantly during this period or they would have no emotion left for the climax. While in the graph this section is often represented by an upward line, the line would be more representative if it was drawn up and down, tending upward, to represent "rising tension" and "falling tension." (In some writing books designated "rising action" and "falling action.")

THE CLIMAX – This is where many beginning writers fail. They skip over the climax, although this is where they have the reader hooked. This is where all the stops are pulled out; where the intensity never slackens; where the reader is eager for every detail. In a short story, the climax is often the longest section of the story. Nevertheless, many of my students have tended to avoid this section.

I had one student whose story set the scene for the climax by introducing a young woman who had no affection or love in her life, deciding to have a baby – someone to love her. This writer described the climax (no pun intended) in one long, run-on sentence: "One night she went to a bar, met a man and went home with him and stayed the night and a month later realized she was pregnant."

Whew! One can almost visualize this writer's relief in getting that scene over with. It is easy to understand why beginning writers are inclined to take this route at the climax, because it is here that the reader gets deeply involved, and here that the writer must therefore become involved.

We are trained, in our society, to stay uninvolved. Children are taught that "big boys (or girls) don't cry." We are inclined to cross the street if we see someone arguing, and we "stay out of it" even when friends or relatives have a quarrel. So one of the things a story writer must learn is to "get into it" when the characters fight or love; to cry unashamedly when writing the sad or emotional parts of their story.

THE DENOUEMENT – (pronounced – DAY nu man). In French it means literally "the untying," but it is best understood as the point where everything that has happened comes together, the point of the story, the outcome, its reason for existence, its meaningful significance.

Why have you, the author-God, chosen to make happen each of the story's events? It had better have been to make a point, and you had better have known what that point was before you started to write the story.

As I mentioned, readers demand that a story "make sense" – that a story not be as chaotic as their own lives.

Stories are about people . . . people with problems. The denouement is the resolution of that problem. Either the main character wins or is defeated by the problem. It is the point to which everything in the story has been leading. And it is just that – a point – often one sentence.

It can also be thought of as the change, the moment when life for the character or characters will never be the same again.

THE ENDING – As you can see by the graph, the ending is short and goes downhill. The story about the main characters is essentially over at the denouement, and no reader likes to have the ending dragged out.

Simply wrap up the loose ends involving the minor characters in a few sentences, and let readers give a sigh of satisfaction as they put the story down.

Often a writer puts in a little twist at the end – an unexpected happening. If the story is light hearted, perhaps a bit of humor to leave the reader smiling; or if it's a sad story, an unexpected bit of tragedy added to bring more tears.

The denouement in a short story usually comes only a paragraph or two from the end. However, in some short-short stories, there is no ending because there are no loose ends to wrap up.

In a novel, the ending is usually the last chapter with the denouement coming at or near the end of the penultimate chapter.

So there you have it. The broad outline within which to fit a story. It will not limit your creativity anymore than will enclosing a painting into a rectangular frame. It will allow your creativity to reach and to move others.

I hope you will use this dramatic form to see how the stories you read fit into the graph. As readers, we do not see the structure because we become caught up in the story, as the author intends. But you should read as a writer reads so you can learn to analyze the structure in order to plan, organize and evaluate your own story.

You will notice I did not say that you will WRITE analytically. Writing – filling that blank page – is creative, but the planning, organizing, evaluating and the REWRITING will use all your powers of analysis.

What They Say

Nothing is more clear than that every plot, worth the name, must be elaborated to its denouement before anything be attempted with the pen. It is only with the denouement constantly in view that we can give a plot its indispensable air of consequence, of causation, by the making of incidents, and especially the tone at all points, tend to the development of the intention.

— Edgar Allen Poe

In a story, you must make up your mind what your point is and stick with it like grim death. That is just another way of saying that it must have form.

— W. Somerset Maugham

Is it enough to be possessed by a feeling in order to express it? Has a drinking song ever been written by a drunken man? It is wrong to think that feeling is everything. In the arts, it is nothing without form.

— Gustave Flaubert

The writer's task is to cleanse, to organize, to articulate the substance of life. Throughout life, there prevails a ghastly absurdity, a frightful raging, such as heredity, inner compulsion, stupidity, malice, profound wickedness. Here we have the Augean Stable which needs to be cleansed over and over again and transformed into a temple.

— Hugo von Hofmannsthal

12   *Putting It All Together*

I will now put these parts together – elements and structure – in a series of story plots, the first of which I will make up as I go along.

Lets take a Western – a Western Romance.

I will start at a moment of tension, a change in circumstance . . . a stagecoach pulls up in a cloud of dust, and because this is a romance, two people are waiting . . . a man and woman (let's not get too modern.)

We must have some character vs. character conflict so I will make the gallant, macho western man, attempt to help the lady with her suitcase. She, a feisty I-can-do-it-myself type (the same character as he: opposites attract, the same types repel), objects strenuously, and as they wrestle with her suitcase, it drops on the man's toe.

What's going to happen next? Well, with a little background (downhill on the graph) we learn they both have to get to the next town by a certain time, although neither knows about the other, and TIME IS RUNNING OUT.

Now we have conflict (him and her) and suspense. Will they make it in time? Will they get together? Because we readers know this is a romance without the writer telling us.

The stagecoach races out of town and into the desert where a wheel comes loose. It must be fixed fast because they have to get to the next town by a certain time. The girl helps over the protestations of the ever-gallant hero. Their quarrel causes the stagecoach to slip off the blocks dropping the wheel on the man's sore toe. More character vs. character conflict.

We can have as many character vs. nature and character vs. character conflicts as we wish. The stagecoach driver gets lost . . . a sandstorm blows in . . . outlaws attack. We can even have one of the passengers secretly determined to stop these two from getting to the next town by a certain time and TIME IS RUNNING OUT. We can have the her-and-him conflict, which is caused by their characters, intensify each of the characters vs. nature conflicts.

What's going to happen next? Are they going to get there on time? Are they going to get together? Of course, we readers know they are going to make it, and in the end get together because this is a simple pot-boiler . . . but how?

Finally, the climax. Indians attack; a prairie fire races towards them; the driver is killed; the stagecoach team is running away; a cliff looms up out of the smoke.

There is no way out!

So . . . she climbs onto the diver's seat with him and drives the team while he chases off the Indians with his six-shooter, then climbs down on the backs of the horses and brings them under control avoiding the cliff. The runaway team has outraced the fire.

Then . . . the denouement.

Just over the hill is the town which they are going to get to in time, thanks to the team running away and due to their heroic efforts. And the two look at each other knowing that by working together they can overcome all obstacles. They have found out they are made for each other which we readers have known all along.

We could even add a little twist to the end and have them discovering they were both trying to get to the town on time for the same reason.

If this was a classic Western, the ending would have him shaking her hand, kissing his horse and riding away into the sunset by himself.

This story has everything – characters who resolve the problems caused by their characters and through their own efforts; conflict, suspense, change. And it follows the dramatic form.

The story line is: Two people in conflict with each other have to overcome obstacles through their own efforts to get to a place by a certain time, and when they get there, their lives are changed. (Keep in mind a story line is not a plot. A story line is a summary of the plot. A plot is ALL the things that happen.)

But this is just a cheap Western, you say. You want to write a literary masterpiece, you say.

Okay. Let's look at a Bible story.

Mary and Joseph

A Roman cop raps at the door and says to Mary: "Yo-all better get down to Bethlehem and pay yo taxes."

Mary, a proper lady who always wants to do the right thing, wrings her hands and says: "But Joseph is off playing cards with the boys and drinking fermented camel's milk. I don't know when he will get home."

"That's yo-alls problem," he says, and rattles off in his armor.

Eventually Joseph gets home and tries to talk her out of going to Bethlehem. But she insists, because it is the proper thing to do. Mary sits on her donkey and grumbling Joseph leads him off into the desert.

So . . . there you have character vs character conflict, and an opening during a tense moment of change. And, of course, suspense. (They have to get to Bethlehem by a certain time, not only to pay their taxes, but because Mary is pregnant.)

Bumbling, inept Joseph wants to take a short cut, but proper Mary insists they take the regular road. He gets them lost; they run out of water; a sandstorm blows up. Joseph wants to give up and turn back, but Mary, feeling the first stirrings, urges him on.

Then the climax. They reach Bethlehem, but THERE IS NO ROOM AT THE INN. Mary, sitting on her donkey, feels the time is now. But passersby pay her no attention. Joseph has disappeared, probably playing cards and drinking fermented camel's milk.

There is no way out!

And then . . . Joseph arrives. The expected appearance of the child has changed him. He wasn't out playing cards and drinking. He was looking for a place for Mary and the child, and he has found it – a manger, and just in the nick of time.

The shepherds arrive, and one of them says: "Yo-all (they are from Southern Israel) know that is the son of God?"

Mary gets a smug look on her face. "I thought it was something like that because Joseph has been impotent ever since he's been drinking that fermented camel's milk."

And Joseph puts his arms around her and the child. He has changed, becoming responsible; and Mary has changed, becoming sweet; and the world has changed, becoming good.

Well, you could tell this as a ribald tale as I did to get your attention, or you could tell it reverently. You could make this story into a movie script as Cecil B. De Mille has, or into a puppet show script and have the little kiddies sitting on the edge of their seats.

Because, it is a GOOD story.

It has wonderful characters, suspense, conflict, change, and it follows the dramatic form. It has abstracted the significant events and organized them into a meaningful significance.

And it's the same story line as the "cheap" Western Romance — two people, in conflict with each other and with nature, overcome terrible obstacles to get to a place by a certain time. When they get there — overcoming through their own efforts the problems created, in part, by their own characters — their lives are changed.

The African Queen

I chose this because it is a great story by a great writer, C. S. Forester; and because it was made into a great movie with great actors, Katherine Hepburn and Humphrey Bogart; and because the movie has appeared on TV numerous times so most of you should be familiar with it.

It starts with the brother of the spinsterish missionary (Rosie) dying. This results in her ending up on a small boat on a river in the middle of the African jungle, in the middle of a war, in company with a drunken Cockney boat captain (Charlie) whose crew has all vanished.

You might think that's almost like Louis L'Amour's prize fighter opening. Can one get more tension than that? Forester can.

This Odd Couple, in obvious conflict with each other, must also overcome their internal conflicts and then overcome the jungle, the river, the enemy; take their tiny craft down a raging, unexplored river; and finally sink a German warship. Whew!

They accomplish all this through their own efforts; first mastering themselves; then the river; then sinking the German ship as the climax; and finally swimming off into the sunset . . . together.

I'm sure you recognize this is the same story line as the other two: Two people, in conflict with themselves and each other, overcome great obstacles to reach a certain place by a certain time and their lives are then changed.

This story line has been used by writers hundreds of times, perhaps thousands. It will be used thousands of times more. I give it to you. It works. In fact, it can be argued there are no more than a dozen or so story lines available. Some argue all those story lines can be found in the Bible stories.

The three examples I have given should make clear to you that each story, despite having the same elements, the same form and the same story line, is completely original. Putting your story into the dramatic form and using all the elements will require all the creativity you can muster, and in the end, it will be original – one that no one else could have written.

And more importantly – it will be read!

What They Say

How do we write a story?

Our own way.

Beyond that, I think it's hard to assign a process to it. There is one great fact that rises up like the Great Divide . . . we all know it, it's this: That the mind in writing a story is in the throes of imagination, and it is not in the calculations of analysis. There is a Great Divide in the workings of the mind – shedding its energy in two directions – it creates in imagination, and it tears down in analysis.

The fact that a story will reduce to elements, can be analyzed, does not necessarily mean it started with them, certainly not consciously. A story can start with a bird song.

— Eudora Welty

. . . You evidently confuse the inspiration, that is, the first instantaneous vision, or emotion in the artist's soul (which is always present) with the WORK.

— Fyodor Doestoevsky in a letter to a friend

PART IV

The Coming Together

13 *No Plain Janes or Wimpy Kenneths*

A fine writing textbook, *The Craft of Fiction* by William C. Knott, mentions *The Maltese Falcon*, one of the first, and still one of the best, private eye stories. The main character is motivated by loyalty – not just our own ordinary commitment to loyalty, but an intense, irrational commitment to loyalty. His partner is killed and the main character's code of loyalty requires that he risk his life to find the killers even though he didn't even like his partner and had been fooling around with his partner's wife. Everything that happens is the result of this characteristic.

Your character must have the ordinary characteristics we all have so that we can relate to the character, but your character must have certain of these characteristics to an intense degree and these various intense characteristics are often in conflict with each other.

A story writer, more than anyone else, must understand that we are all one. Despite culture or color, we all have universal feelings. A Haitian cries the same as does an American and for the same reasons. At the same time, each person in the world is unique. We must build our characters like that. They must have human characteristics – be types – and at that same time be marvelously individual.

One author explained: "When I start out with a type, I always end up with an individual. And when I start with an individual, I end up with a type."

The more we readers can relate to your characters' humanity, and the stronger their individual characteristics, the more moving and stronger your story will be. *Gone With the Wind* would not be a memorable story if Scarlett had just an ordinary self-centeredness, in conflict with an ordinary will.

Characters Must Have Substance

Story people, like real people, are both born and made. We are who we are primarily because of who our parents are, who their parents were and which society we are born into. Perhaps we add a few touches of individuality to our makeup from our experiences as we grow up, but that's all.

In real life, we get to know our friends better and better as we get to know their background. Where did they come from? Who were their parents? Grandparents?

And we get to know ourselves better and better as we get to know and understand our own parents and grandparents – when we understand where we came from.

You must understand the characters in your story, and to do this I strongly suggest you write a narrative, giving your major characters parents, grandparents and great-grandparents – that every major character has a reason contained in this background for each of his major character traits.

A novel I wrote has seven major characters, and I wrote a multi-page analysis of each before starting. Therefore, the characters were quite well developed in my mind to start with because I had put in several weeks living with them, but they grew and even changed during the writing of the book as I got to know them even better.

Round People and Flat People

The chief difference between major and minor characters is their unexpectedness or lack of it. The reader does not know how the major character (round, multi-dimensional) is going to act in any given circumstance, especially at the beginning of the story. It's part of the suspense, the what's-going-to-happen-next.

The author knows, for the most part, but even the author and sometimes the character is surprised at their reaction. Minor characters (flat, one-dimensional) always act in one, predictable way – that's their reason for existence in the story.

For example, how is the main character in my book, who has never been on a horse in her life, going to react when a young man she is attracted to asks her to go horseback riding and then asks her if she can ride? Well, you, as the author, know she was raised in a family with five strong-willed, aggressive brothers, and if she had ever shown a moment of weakness, or if she had said she couldn't do something they could do, they would have teased her unmercifully. So, how do you think she answered? (And the response leads to a very funny scene.) The reader, also, gets to know these background details about her in due time.

A minor character in my book is of a type I hate. He is the security officer for an apartment building. He can only follow the rules; can't think for himself and delights in throwing his authority around.

It is necessary for the plot that my main character thwart him at a key point in the story, so as foreshadowing I have half-a-dozen scenes where my heroine gets around him, because, of course, she hates his type also. Actually it's very simple. My heroine knows the only security the rent-a-cop really values is his own security, so a threat to his job always brings him around. He is perfectly predictable and the story depends on it.

The villain in my book does terrible things to several of the main characters, but I like her anyhow. And perhaps the readers do also. I have given her a background that makes her actions, as awful as they are, perfectly logical. She could do nothing else. However, her actions are a huge surprise and only make sense when the reader is made aware of her background. She has more than one dimension to her character because she starts off appearing to be sweet and charming, and she is always strong and interesting.

Whether you are writing a short story or a novel, I recommend strongly that you first spend considerable time getting to know your characters – going back up to three generations – and writing it all down.

As a literary critic said about Chekhov's characters: "He has lived with his people as well as looked at them through a window."

What's In a Name?

Mucho. In our culture, we get our names before anyone knows anything about us. A boy may be given a strong, masculine name like "Wolfgang" even though when he grows up he turns out to be a wimp, and probably should have a name like "Ashley."

The North American Indians have the right idea. They give a baby a baby's name, and then the child, when growing up, chooses a name based on an image of themselves.

While the name chosen may be a bit ambitious, like "Thunder Hawk," it at least gives something to try and live up to. The Crow Indians' greatest chief, as a young man, named himself "Plenty Coups" meaning that he would have many accomplishments – and he lived up to that name.

You, as writers, have the opportunity to give your characters their names after they have already grown up and developed their unique characteristics. Don't waste that opportunity. Think long and hard about it.

I wanted my main character to be as strong and aggressive as any woman would be who, to survive her childhood, had to compete with five strong-willed brothers. But I also wanted her to have many contrasts and conflicts in her character to give her more than one dimension. For example, while at the time of the story she is in a sophisticated environment as an assistant on a New York City magazine, she was raised in the earthy environment of an Oregon lumber camp. Her parents were European immigrants, and the name I gave her was Hannah. To me the name evokes simple Old World values, and contrasts and conflicts with her present sophisticated and superficial life style. To the hero, a mystery man, I gave a mysterious name – Armenian.

The villain I gave two short, and to my ears, raspy names – Nydia Carlson. It would not be appropriate, I thought, to give her a melodious name like Penelope. To another major character, a ranch wife who was formerly an English teacher, I gave a literary name – Rebecca. To a minor character, a cowboy who only speaks when he has something to say, I gave a plain name – Frank.

Perhaps the above examples give you an idea of the kind of thinking that goes into deciding on names for your characters.

Keeping the Characters Straight

Not long ago I started an English mystery novel, but quit after one chapter. Each of the characters had four-or five-syllable names – Chestermirshire, Fotheringhamton, etc. I was lost almost immediately. I could never remember which was which.

You must choose names that will be memorable, that fit the characters (at least in your mind) and that are individual. Just think for a moment of names of athletic stars – Cassius Clay, Mohammed Ali, The Great One, Yurri Curri, Theoren Fleury.

Although you can't "borrow" names of famous people, you should come up with some names at least as unique and memorable.

Call some of your characters by nicknames, some by their initials, some by their last name (as in Smith of *Breaking Smith's Quarter Horse*), some by their two names. Use any trick to make sure that the reader will recognize the character even if the character doesn't appear again for several pages or chapters.

You can get ideas for names from the phone book, from the rosters of professional sports, from people you have known in the past. You can mix and match them, make them euphonious or grating, short or long, unique or common (but not too many of the latter and certainly not for your main characters.) Come up with names like Scarlett O'Hara, Rhett Butler, or the wimp, Ashley Wilkes. Avoid "cute" spellings – Jayne is still plain Jane when pronounced.

What They Say

Writers have a little trick. People think writers take their characters from life. They do not. What they do is find some man or woman who, for some obscure reason, arouses their interest. Such a man or woman is invaluable to a writer. He takes the few facts he knows and tries to build a whole life. People are starting places for him and when he gets through, often enough, what results has little or nothing to do with the person he started with.

– Sherwood Anderson

14 *A Review of Elements and Structure*

Let us review the elements and structure of stories and then examine A.B. Guthrie Jr.'s *The Big IT* in the Appendix and see if this Pulitzer-Prize-winning-author knows how to tell a story.

For all practical purposes every story contains *characters* – strong, fascinating characters, not wimps. These characters are in *conflict* within themselves, with each other and with nature. These conflicts must be built into the characters and into the situation in which they find themselves, and what follows will be *suspense* and eventually a dramatic *change* in their lives and the lives of those around them.

One other element all stories must have is a point, usually called a *theme*, although the word "theme" seems to frighten some students. I will be examining it in a subsequent chapter.

Again, *The African Queen* with Katherine Hepburn, the old maid missionary, and Humphrey Bogart, the drunken, shiftless boat captain, makes a good review of the required elements. Put those two characters in the situation of being together in a small boat in the middle of an African river in the middle of a war, and you <u>are</u> going to have conflict, suspense and change – you couldn't avoid it if you tried.

It must be clear from this example that it is up to you, the author, to build your characters and devise the situation so that the other elements of a story follow.

And now the structure. It's a five-part structure – *Beginning, Middle, Climax, Denouement* and *End*.

At this point, read *The Big IT* in the appendix and examine its elements and structure. (This is a short-short story and the elements will not be developed to the extent they would be in a longer work.)

CHARACTERS – Two Plumes, the not easily impressed Piegan Chief, who may or may not be thinking about wiping out the little town of Fort Benton.
The narrator, clearly a backwoodsman coming into town for a little fun along with all the other characters living on the frontier.

CONFLICT – The conflict between Whites and Indians.

THE SITUATION – Whites decide to impress Indians by firing a small cannon at a hillside.

SUSPENSE – Will they succeed in firing the cannon? Will it impress the Indians? Will the narrator survive?

CHANGE – Whites discover Indians not easily impressed. Indians discover White men are even crazier than they have always suspected. (Denouement)

THEME – When two cultures don't understand each other, they do silly things.

This is, as Guthrie explains in his foreword, a true incident. I have heard this incident myself, and a number of western writers have taken the incident and made a story out of it in their own way. The incident is that the Fort Benton residents decided to impress the Indians by firing a cannon ball into a hillside, but the mule the small canon was loaded on started to buck and the cannon shot the ball into the ground at the mule's feet instead.

That's the incident. What did Guthrie do? What every story writer does – he added characters, conflict, suspense, change and theme. And he told the story in the dramatic form – beginning, middle, climax, denouement. (There is no need for an end as there are no loose ends to wrap up.)

You might ask: "Did Guthrie take a writing course to learn these aspects of writing stories?"

My answer: "Who knows?" and "What does it matter?"

Guthrie may have taken a writing course, or he may be a "natural" writer – that is, he may be a great reader and he may have an analytical mind which allows him to understand how the stories he reads are constructed. But it doesn't matter if one has learned these basic elements and structure of story writing subconsciously or consciously as long as one knows them. They are as fundamental to story telling as putting the punch line at the end is fundamental to joke telling.

I expect you to make use of these basic elements. When you are organizing a story in your head or on paper, think about these elements and structure.

When you have written a story, examine it.

Maybe you have put in too much background; maybe the beginning doesn't occur at a moment of tension, a change of circumstance; maybe you have skipped too briefly over the climax; maybe the denouement is not clearly defined; maybe you have gone astray and not kept to the theme; maybe your characters are weak.

Now that you know the structure and the basic elements, you have measuring devices to judge the effectiveness of your story. USE THEM.

15 *High Noon for All You Writers*

The beginning for a story writer, and also for a story reader, is character. One might think that a story is a series of happenings, but that is only half of the equation – who it's happening to is the other half.

Events in the abstract such as a typhoon in Bangladesh, a famine in Somalia, a massacre in Rwanda, mean practically nothing to us. Certainly they do not affect us, unless by some chance someone we know is involved in these events.

And it's the same for a story.

So, we start with character. There are ways of getting an idea for a story that I mention elsewhere, such as starting from a "theme" or starting from an incident. But even if one of these is the seed for your story, the very first thing you have to do is add characters.

There are few rules as to who your characters might be. Steinbeck, for example, in *Cannery Row*, *Tortilla Flat* and *Sweet Thursday,* wrote about a bunch of Monterey, California, bums living in flop houses, or on the beach, or in one case, an abandoned boiler which had been used to generate steam to cook the sardines canned on cannery row.

However, there is one inviolable rule.

Your main character MUST NOT be a wimp. We know enough whiners in real life – may even be one ourselves. We want to read about a person who has control over his/her life, and perhaps the lives of those around them – a person who can make tough decisions when faced with a problem, not like you and I who tend to wait for the problem to go away.

A character can, sometimes, start out *appearing* as a wimp and change, but the strong character that the wimp becomes must be already present. The change to a strong character (or any change) must not be miraculous, but be present, indicated by foreshadowing and *revealed* through your art of storytelling.

Your character MUST have a problem, and that problem MUST be an outgrowth of the character's character. And because the character is not a wimp, the character will either solve the problem or be defeated by the problem through your protagonist's own actions and decisions – not some intervention by God, or fate, or chance, or some other person. The problem has to be a universal problem, that is, one that faces all humans. In that way, every reader can relate to it.

A classic western tale has a "strong man" whose word is his bond, who is hired by the "good people," despite his reluctance to put on the marshal's badge, to protect them from the "bad people." When the bad people gang up on him he asks for help, but all the good people refuse, leaving him to face all the bad guys at once . . . alone.

This would be no problem for a man whose character did not put great emphasis on being "a man of his word." He could just run away and say: "I didn't want to be marshal in the first place."

But for this character, it's a tremendous problem.

He's either going to be killed if he insists on keeping his word to protect the good people who have abandoned him, or he is going to live the rest of his life knowing he is a man who cannot be depended on to keep his word.

What does he do? What's going to happen? It's a good story line, one that's been used countless times and will be used countless times again.

The classic tale with this story line is "High Noon," a reference to the gun fight which is going to take place at high noon. It's going to be a gunfight between him, and all the bad guys.

His wife, whom he has just married and whom he loves dearly says: "But what about me? Don't you love me?" He shrugs his shoulders.

His best friend refuses to help him and urges that he run away. He has lost his wife, lost his best friend and lost all the "good" people of the town. Why not leave?

But he refuses to go back on his word even in the face of abandonment and his possible death.

What happens next? Read the story.

And it's a good story because we can all relate to the hero. We all face, at one time or another, our High Noons when we must decide whether or not to stand up for what we believe in and facing the consequences, or to give in, be a wimp, and say something like: "To get along, one must go along."

Character is Plot

A story cannot exist without characters. It would only be an incident.

Barbara Taylor Bradford explained:

Graham Greene said that character is plot. That clarifies the whole art of fiction writing to me. It is the character of the main protagonist that shapes and animates the plot.

Like Bradford, you also must understand this. (She has sold 25 million of her books in the English language alone, while they have been translated and sold in 18 other languages). When the thunder rolls and the lightning strikes and you are smashed right between the eyes with the understanding that *character is plot* then you will have made a major step in becoming a story writer.

I will do my best to help bring this understanding to you, but first I should again define "plot."

A plot is the things that happen.

You will remember that in another section I gave you three story lines. A story line is the summary of a plot.

You will recall that the story line was the same in all three stories – the western romance, the bible story of Mary and Joseph and the African Queen adventure – two people in conflict with each other, in conflict with themselves, in conflict with nature have to get somewhere by a certain time and when they get there, their lives are changed.

But the plot, the actual things that happened in each of the stories, was completely different – because they were happening to different characters.

So, character is plot. The things that happen, happen because of the character, and they reveal character. If a happening in your story, no matter how thrilling it might be, is not caused by the character of your protagonist, or does not reveal anything about the character of the protagonist, you must throw it out.

Let me give you an example. A man walking home from church one Sunday finds a sack full of money in a ditch. So what is the problem?

Let us imagine he is the minister and he had just finished giving a sermon on honesty. And let us give this man an overwhelming commitment to honesty, perhaps instilled in him by his father. Now, you may say, we have a problem. Not really. Because of his character he will simply turn the money over to the proper authorities.

However, let us imagine that he has a son, the light of his life, whom he loves with great passion, perhaps because he himself had not received any love from his father. And let us imagine that to save the son's life he must have an operation in the U.S. which costs a lot of money, in fact, the amount of money in the sack.

Now he's got a problem.

How are you, the writer, going to solve this conflict between two facets of his character? You could have him turn the money in, and the owner is so grateful and impressed with his honesty that he gives him the money he needs to save his son. But that would not work. It would be someone else solving the problem. No, the character must solve it himself. Perhaps you will give him still another facet of his character that allows him to solve the problem. Or, perhaps he will be defeated by it, and you will have written a tragedy.

Perhaps . . . well, you're the writer. It's up to you to come up with the happenings that will allow the character to solve it. Character is plot. Character must determine what happens.

Let us examine Scarlett O'Hara in *Gone With the Wind*. Scarlett is a spoiled brat. Not just an ordinary spoiled brat, but an incredibly spoiled brat, and she loses the man she loves because of this character.

"What is going to happen to me?" she says.

"Frankly, my dear, I don't give a damn!" he says. Her father, before he dies, and understanding her hidden strength of character, tells her to take care of Tara, the ancestral home. But the soldiers come and destroy Tara. I only remember the story vaguely but I remember the scene where her maid says:

"Oh, Miss Scarlett, what are we going to do?"

And Scarlett responds:

"We are going to get to work."

This is at the end of Part I. The crucible of the Civil War has revealed another facet of Scarlett's character – one, however, already present and planted in our mind by foreshadowing.

And Book II deals with this new character – an almost fanatic strength of will which both causes her problems and will either solve the problems that arise, or end in tragic defeat. Character is plot.

16 *The Craft of Characterization*

Characters, especially minor characters in your story, should be as deftly dissected as a surgeon removing a sty . . . and then they should be immediately put into action demonstrating what you have said about them.

Readers do not like long-winded descriptions of any of the characters – particularly not their appearance – even the major ones. Write a few choice words describing the key aspects of their appearance, and leave the rest to the reader's imagination. Readers will have their own mental image of the character. Then, let the facets of their character be *revealed* by their actions. Here is a minor character in *A River Runs Through It* neatly scalpeled by Norman Maclean:

> *He was last off the train, and he came down the platform trying to remember what he thought an international-cup tennis player looked like. He undoubtedly was the first and last passenger ever to step off a Great Northern coach car at Wolf Creek, Montana, wearing white flannels and two sweaters.*

Here's Maclean again with his scalpel:

> *On the crate at the other end of the bar was a female character known as Old Rawhide to the goats up and down the Great Northern line. About 10 years before, at a Fourth of July celebration she had been elected beauty queen of Wolf Creek. She had ridden bareback standing up through the 111 inhabitants, mostly male, who had lined one of Wolf Creek's two streets. Her skirts flew high, and she won the contest. But, since she didn't quite have what it takes to become a professional rider, she did the next best thing. However, she still wore the divided skirts of a western horsewoman of the day, although they must have been a handicap in her new profession.*

From John Steinbeck in *Cannery Row*:

Mack was the elder, leader, mentor, and to a small extent the exploiter of a little group of men who had in common no families, no money, and no ambitions beyond food, drink and contentment. But whereas most men in their search for contentment destroy themselves and fall wearily short of their targets, Mack and his friends approached contentment casually, quietly and absorbed it gently.

From Joseph Conrad in *Lord Jim*:

. . . He was gentlemanly, steady, tractable, with a thorough knowledge of his duties; and in time, when yet very young, he became chief mate of a fine ship, without ever having been tested by those events of the sea that show in the light of day the inner worth of a man, the edge of his temper, and the fibre of his stuff; that reveal the quality of his resistance and the secret truth of his pretences, not only to others but also to himself.

(What makes us think he is soon going to be tested?)

In each of the above examples, the authors then put their characters in action showing the attributes that have been suggested.

To illustrate the last point is John Irving in *The Water Method Man*:

*It was then, Merrill claims, that the American couple drove up in their new Porsche. They were apparently lost; they thought they had come to the ski races in Zell. The man, **a frightened one**, rolled up his window and stared with considerable insecurity at the yelling crowd on the bank. But the man's wife, **big and fortyish**, with a jutting chin, slammed her door and strode around to her husband's side of the car. (My emphasis.)*

"Well, dammit," she said to him, forcing him to roll down the window. "You and your rotten German and lousy sense of directions. We're late. We've missed the first event."

"Madam," Merrill said to her as he dragged me past them, "be glad that the first event missed you."

As has been said: "Characters without action are lame; action without characters blind."

17   *Princes or Paupers?*

Many books and stories of earlier generations were written with Kings and Princes and "knights in shining armour" as the heroes, but today's authors most often choose characters from the more ordinary walks of life.

That is not to say, however, that the characters are ordinary even though we readers find it easy to relate to them.

Paul St. Pierre (a newspaper columnist in Vancouver in addition to being author of *Breaking Smith's Quarter Horse*) explains why he wrote about Smith, a small rancher in the Chilcotin:

The movers and shakers . . . tend to be nervous and uncertain men, more concerned about what others think of them than what they think of themselves. More often than not they are, truth to tell, a bit dull. And if you write about dull people you will write a dull book.

W. Somerset Maugham wrote in his memoirs *The Summing Up*:

Kings, dictators, commercial magnates are from our point of view very unsatisfactory . . . They cannot be made real. The ordinary is the writer's richer field. Its unexpectedness, its singularity, its infinite variety afford unending material. The great man is too often all of a piece; it is the little man that is a bundle of contradictory elements. For my part, I would much sooner spend a month on a desert island with a veterinary surgeon than with a prime minister.

For myself, as a newspaperman, the people I have often had to write about, who were considered in the usual sense "a success," have had such a single-minded purpose to their lives that there is no conflict or suspense with which to make a story.

However, if you choose an "ordinary" character to write about, make sure that he (or she) is "extraordinary" in some qualities, and it will be those qualities which determine the plot.

Luigi Pirandello wrote in *Six Characters in Search of an Author*:

When the characters are really alive before their author, the latter does nothing but follow them in their action, in their words, in the situations which they suggest to him. When a character is born, he acquires at once such an independence, even of his own author, that he can be imagined by everybody even in many other situations where the author never dreamed of placing him; and so he acquires for himself a meaning which the author never thought of giving him.

Elsewhere, I have suggested that you write a narrative of your main characters going back three generations and giving them a basis for each of their main characteristics. I did that for my novel. At the same time, I wrote a narrative of the plot; wrote out the theme in one sentence, and had fixed in my mind the scene containing the denouement.

This may sound like a straight jacket, but as I came to know the characters even better, I discovered, as Pirandello points out, that the characters took on a life of their own; they behaved in unexpected ways, and new plot twists presented themselves. (Nevertheless, I kept my mind firmly on the theme.)

I came to love my characters, even the villain. I still do. I know them better than anyone I have ever known. It was one of the wonderful things about writing a novel.

What They Say

. . . Homo Sapiens and Homo Fictus. Homo Fictus is more elusive than his cousin. He is created in the minds of hundreds of different novelists, who have conflicting methods of gestation, so one must not generalize. Still, one can say a little about him. He is generally born off (stage), and capable of dying on. He wants little food or sleep, he is tirelessly occupied with human relationships. And – most important – we can know more about him than we can know about any of our fellow creatures, because his creator and narrator are one.

– E. M. Forster

18 *Theme: What Your Story Is About*

"Theme" is a word nearly as abstract as the word "love," and nearly as vague. It is a concept my students have had great difficulty understanding. It is easier to say what it isn't, rather than what it is.

Theme is not a "great truth." After all, after you have used up the Ten Commandments, how many "great truths" are left? It is not a "message" or a "moral." If you want to send a message, fax it or use Western Union.

Theme is "what the story is about." Its "meaningful significance." It is the unifying thread which ties together everything that happens and everything that is said.

As a writer, why do you choose one thing to happen and not another? Because what you choose helps tell the story. That's why.

Obviously, then, you must clearly understand what your story is about. One way to accomplish this is to put your theme into one simple, complete sentence. If your theme is vague, as it would be in a phrase such as "the problems of life," your story will be vague. And if you require a long-winded paragraph to state your theme, then "what your story is about" will also be fuzzy.

To bring the abstraction down to earth, I will examine theme in two well-known stories – Hemingway's *The Old Man and the Sea* and Steinbeck's *The Pearl*.

In Hemingway's story, the old man, a fisherman all his life, has not caught a fish for 84 days. Finally, he accomplishes an incredible victory and attains a great dream. He has caught the greatest fish in the world after a magnificent battle lasting several days.

Then, as he is returning with his prize, towing it behind the boat, the sharks arrive and tear it to pieces.

I think the theme could be written: "Some people are jealous of success and they (the sharks) will arrive to tear us down at the moment of our greatest victory." Or, perhaps, "The greater your success, the more likely someone (or something) will try to destroy it." Or, perhaps, "To attain your dream is to lose it." Other analysts and readers may come up with different conclusions, or different ways of putting it.

But as Albert J. Guerard says in his introduction to Joseph Conrad's *The Secret Sharer*:

> *Every great work of art operates on multiple levels of meaning and suasion. And a work of art as general as* The Secret Sharer, *and as personal, may have something very particular to say to every new reader.*

In *The Pearl*, Steinbeck used precisely the same theme. The poor pearl fisherman finds the "pearl of the world." What happens next? You guessed it. "The sharks" come in the person of the pearl buyers who try to cheat him out of it, and the thieves and murderers who hunt him and his family down, eventually killing his baby who is more important to him than the "pearl of the world." He throws it back into the ocean. He was defeated, but in Hemingway's story, the "old man" wins.

In one movie version of *The Old Man and the Sea*, the movie maker also drew a clear analogy with the life of Christ.

One of the movie scenes shows Anthony Quinn, after his epic battle to land the fish and his loss to the sharks, staggering up the beach in defeat dragging the mast and sail of his boat in an almost precise image of Christ carrying his cross through the streets of Jerusalem. The analogy is well taken because Christ had astonishing success with his preaching, and the established priests – the sharks – convinced the Romans to crucify him.

The movie carries the Christ analogy even further. When the Old Man arrives on shore with the skeleton of the fish, he tells the boy (his disciple) that he was defeated. And then he tells of his great struggle with the fish. The other fishermen in the village arrive, listen to the story, and tell the Old Man he is still their leader; that he has caught the "fish of the world." It doesn't matter about the sharks. Perhaps one can see these events as a mirror of Christ's defeat on the cross, and his eventual victory.

The Old Man and the Sea is a great piece of literature, not because the theme is a "great truth," but because anyone in any society in any generation can relate to it. The Old Man's experience was a human experience, as was Christ's.

Don't think that because this theme has already been used that it can't be used again. There are only a limited number of themes, and it would be a waste of your time to try and come up with an original one. (If the theme were original, it would have to be outside the experience of any reader, and therefore no one could relate to it. The story would not show the essential humanity of man.) According to author Eudora Welty:

Whatever our theme in writing, it is old and tried. Whatever our place, it has been visited by the stranger, it will never be new again. It is only the vision that can be new; but that is enough.

One can often get an idea about the theme of a story by the title the author chose.

For example, Steinbeck's *East of Eden* comes from the biblical story of Cain and Abel. "And Cain went out from the presence of the Lord, and dwelt in the land of Nod, on the <u>east of</u> Eden." His title *The Grapes of Wrath* comes from the biblical story in Isaiah which refers to God's wrath when the Israelites do not follow the laws. Isaiah states God caused the vineyards to grow wild in punishment for this failure to keep the laws.

In Europe it is the custom in small villages to toll the church bell when a local person dies. It would not be uncommon for someone, hearing the bell, to ask "for whom the bell tolls?" John Donne wrote,: "No man is an Iland, intire of it selfe; every man is a peece of the Continent...Any man's death diminishes me. And therefore never send to know <u>for whom the bell tolls</u>; it tolls for thee." Hence, Hemingway's *For Whom the Bell Tolls*.

Steinbeck's *Of Mice and Men* comes from the Robbie Burns line: "The best laid schemes <u>of mice and men</u> often go astray." And, of course, that is what the story is about. Although a reader can extract different ideas from the story, it is clearly the thread Steinbeck used in his own mind to tie the story's events together.

19 *Point of View and "Voice"*

When you sit down at your desk to write your story – to fill that blank page – you first have some decisions to make. I've already suggested you have a narrative description and background of your characters; a plot narrative that takes you to the denouement, and a theme clearly in your mind, if not down on paper.

And now you must decide on the point of view and the "voice" you will take.

You have many points of view and an infinity of "voices" to choose from, but there is one absolute: You must stick with your choice and not jump about.

You can choose the point of view of God looking down from above and telling what's happening as each of the characters see it, experience it, interpret it – the omniscient.

You can show your story through the eyes of a "narrator," a character on the edge or outside the events of the main characters in the story.

You can show the story from the point of view of one character, the main character – the "assigned" point of view.

In rare circumstances, you can show part of the story from one character's viewpoint and then change to another.

You can show the story in the third person: "He" or "She," or in the first person, "I." You can show the story in the present tense or the past tense (but rarely the former.)

There are others, but these are the major ones. All have their advantages and pitfalls.

How do you decide?

To make that decision, I believe you have to first determine what it is you hope to accomplish with your story. Are you trying to impress people with your wonderful words or your insights? Do you want readers to say: "Wow, look at him (or her) write?"

Or are you trying to get the reader involved with your story – "to project it in such a way that it becomes part of the experience of the person who reads it," as Hemingway said.

In my opinion, the only successful approach is the desire to get the reader involved.

The quickest and most direct way to do that is to show the story through only one designated set of eyes, and to make that person the "I."

However, it's a bit tricky to write sentences and paragraphs that are not full of the letter "I." It's a bit easier to designate a set of eyes in the third person – he or she.

With a narrator you are putting another person between the reader and the story; and with the "God" approach you are in danger of "telling" the story, rather than "showing" it through action and dialogue.

With the "assigned" view you are limited to scenes where your assigned character is present. But you are the writer and you can have anything happen you want, so this is not usually a big problem.

In any case, with the "assigned" view, either first person or third person, the story is revealed to the reader at the same time it is revealed to the assigned character. The author *must* stay out of it.

If you must have a scene when your character is not present, you have to move to another viewpoint, but this is hard on the reader who has become involved in your first set of eyes. Therefore, it should be allowed to happen rarely, if at all.

But it can be done. The transition "Meanwhile, back at the ranch . . .", famous in Western pot-boilers, is clearly going to be seen through a different set of eyes than the scene just completed. Another way to handle it is have another character tell the "assigned" character what happened "back at the ranch."

Another problem with the assigned approach is how is your character going to describe what they look like? It can only be done by some obvious trickery such as seeing himself (or herself) in the mirror or a reflection in a pool of water, and then describing what they see. But your readers are forgiving as long as they continue to want to know what is going to happen next.

In any case, I've already recommended that you do not indulge yourself in lengthy physical descriptions of your characters. Readers prefer to use their imagination, but you must give them a starting point.

I recommend that, until you become familiar with your choices, you choose the assigned, third person, past tense point of view.

"Voice" is a bit more vague. Professors have written a number of books on the subject, mostly of an abstract nature.

It's easiest to understand from examples.

Steinbeck, in writing *The Pearl*, used a simple, child-like "voice," with a touch of the mystical and the musical in it. I recommend you read it to see what I mean.

In Guthrie's *The Big IT*, (reproduced in the Appendix) he used a story-teller's "voice," rich in primitive emotions and earthy metaphors. A reader can imagine sitting around a campfire while an old Mountain Man tells this story.

Every story has its own "voice" so it would be ridiculous for me to recommend to you which one to use.

Whatever point of view and "voice" you decide on I urge you to stick with it like a fly to flypaper until the story is finished.

In the meantime, when you read, make note of the point of view and the "voice" the author is using. The examples in the Appendix illustrate several different points of view while each takes on a different "voice."

20 *Openings and the Subliminal*

At the very opening a writer must make an immediate and intimate contact with his story. For this reason, I confess, I tend to judge most of the stories I read by the opening sentences. When I say this I am not thinking of beauty of phrase, or the rhythm of the sentences, or anything of that sort. I am thinking only of this one kind of effectiveness: do we strike the key-note at once?

— Sean O'Faolain

Subliminal knowledge – the knowledge we have that we don't necessarily know from where it came – plays an important role in reading stories.

For example, here is the opening paragraph of *Treasure of the Sierra Madre*. (The book by B. Traven never attained great popularity, but it became a classic movie starring John Huston and Humphrey Bogart.)

The bench on which Dobbs was sitting was not so good. One of the slats was broken; the one next to it was bent so that to have to sit on it was a sort of punishment. If Dobbs deserved punishment, or if this punishment was being inflicted upon him unjustly, as most punishments are, such a thought did not entered his head at this moment. He would have noticed that he was sitting uncomfortably only if someone had asked him if he was comfortable. Nobody, of course, bothered to question him.

What have you learned? Who do you often find sitting on a bench? Where is the bench?

Perhaps you, the reader, get the impression that here is a bum sitting on a park bench. Emphasizing this impression is that nobody, *of course*, questioned him to ask if he was uncomfortable.

(How many homeless people have you asked lately if they were uncomfortable?)

Why didn't Dobbs notice he was uncomfortable? Probably had something more important on his mind. A bit of foreshadowing here; the suggestion of a problem. In any case, it is certainly an opening at a tense moment – a moment of change.

Whew! That's a lot to learn in four sentences. But the reader gets all this, at least on a subconscious level.

Wouldn't it have been awful if the author had then EXPLAINED all the above to us?

Did the author "strike the key-note at once," as O'Faolain asks? Well, this is certainly not going to be a story about high society. In fact, this is a story about greed and gold in the jungles of Mexico, and this opening paragraph seems to fit such a story.

Readers may not consciously analyze the information contained in the above paragraph, but readers do receive this information in their minds subliminally. You, as a writer, must be aware of this.

While the reader will receive great gobs of subliminal information from anything you write, you as the writer must take a considerably more conscious approach. That is why I urge you to analyze as you read, but keeping in mind the reader, as a rule, does not do this.

So let's read some openings. See if they turn you on – make you want to find out what is going to happen next. At the same time, try to view these openings analytically, from the point of view of a writer trying to "strike the keynote at once!"

I'm choosing these openings from one book, an anthology titled *Southwest Fiction*, edited by Max Apple. They are not selected as examples of the best or the worst, but probably about the average – which is to say, good, because any successful author devotes a great amount of effort, thinking and rethinking to the opening.

My Real Estate by Max Apple

I have always believed in property. Though a tenant now, I have prospects. In fact, Joanne Williams, my Realtor, thinks I have the greatest prospects in the world. She has always dropped in on me now and then, but these days she comes up almost every time she leaves her seat for popcorn or a Coke. She brings her refreshment with her and she refreshes me. She has done so right from the start, ever since I first realized that I really wanted to own my own home.

I Bought a Little City by Donald Barthelme

So I bought a little city (it was Galveston, Texas) and told everybody that nobody had to move, we were going to do it just gradually, very relaxed, no big changes overnight. They were pleased and suspicious.

Would you like to know what happens next? Is the main character named "Ross Perot?"

The Gay Place by William Brammer

The country is most barbarously large and final. It is too much country – boondock country – alternately drab and dazzling, spectral and remote. It is so wrongfully muddled and various that it is difficult to conceive of it as all of a piece. Though it begins simply enough, as a part of the other.

The Bronc People by William Eastlake

The two quiet Indians, resting in Z shapes, could watch and hear the shots going back and forth, back and forth, as in a Western movie. But suddenly someone was hurt and it wasn't like a Western movie now.

Whew! I want to know what's going to happen next. (Note how obvious it is, without saying so, that this is set in modern times.)

The Last Running by John Graves

They called him Pajarito, in literal trader Spanish interpretation of his surname, or more often Tom Tejano, since he had been in those early fighting days before the Texans had flooded up onto the plains in such numbers that it became no longer practical to hate them with specificity.

What kind of a story do you think this going to be? Next is the opening of a story by one my favorite authors.

Lost Sister, by Dorothy M. Johnson

Our household was full of women, who overwhelmed my Uncle Charlie and sometimes confused me with their bustle and chatter. We were the only men on the place. I was nine years old when still another woman came – Aunt Bessie, who had been living with the Indians.

Here is an opening by Louis L'Amour. Many people like to deride L'Amour, but he sold one million copies of every book he wrote. Maybe he knew something about story writing.

The Strong Shall Live by Louis L'Amour

The land was fire beneath and the sky was brass above, but throughout the day's long riding the bound man sat erect in the saddle and cursed them for thieves and cowards. Their blows did not silence him, although the blood from his swollen and cracked lips had dried on his face and neck.

Wow! As you can see, Louis L'Amour follows the advice that he gives to beginning writers about how to start a story: "Shoot the sheriff on the first page." In this particular story we might surmise that the sheriff was shot even before the first page.

Here's another of the modern authors whom I admire. This is from a chapter in his book (which became an Oscar-winning movie).

Terms of Endearment by Larry McMurtry

Royce Dunlop was lying in bed with a cold can of beer balanced on his stomach. The phone by the bed began to ring and he reached over and picked the receiver up without disturbing the can of beer. He had a big stomach, and it was no real trick to balance a can of beer on it, but in this instance the can was sitting precisely over his navel, and keeping it there while talking on the phone was at least a little bit of a trick.

What kind of man does this opening suggest?

The Woman in the Green House
by **Durango Mendoza**

> *He came on horseback, riding slowly up the dirt road from the corner, his old saddle creaking and his body swaying slightly with the gait. The horse's hooves chipped rough crescents into the hard earth beneath the layer of dust with clopping sounds, and it began to plod slower until it stopped before the small green tar paper house.*

A romance? Why did the horse go slower and then stop at this place? Been there before? Why do we think this story takes place in a town? Because the horse and horseman turn a corner. Lots of information here – probably mostly subliminal as far as the reader is concerned. In any case, our curiosity has been whetted.

Here's a good one.

My Brother is a Cowboy by **Carolyn Osborn**

> *My daddy used to advise my brother and me, "Don't tell everything you know." This was his golden rule. I keep it in mind as I constantly disregard it. I've been busy most of my life telling everything I know.*

I'll close this chapter by citing a classic opening from literature by Franz Kafka:

From *The Metamorphosis:*

> *As Gregor Samsa awoke one morning from uneasy dreams, he found himself transformed in his bed into a gigantic insect.*

21 *Writing the Opening Scene*

A common problem for story writers is writing several pages, or several chapters, and then discovering we have reached the beginning.

It seems to be a writer's affliction. For some reason, we seem to feel we have to PREPARE the reader for the beginning.

Perhaps it is US we are preparing.

Some tricks may be in order to save yourself from this embarrassment.

I have explained there are three elements to a scene – description of setting, description of action and dialogue.

An opening scene has those three elements in addition to three more: it must establish the <u>time and place</u>; <u>introduce the main character</u>; <u>suggest the problem</u>.

You will find these three elements in the opening scenes of most, if not all, stories you read, and a fine example of this is Steinbeck's opening for *Of Mice and Men* which I recommend you read and analyze.

In previous ages, novels took a more roundabout approach to the beginning. But today's reader (probably including you) will not sit still for a novel or short story, or movie script that doesn't get "right into it."

The trick is knowing where IT is.

I've already mentioned that Louis L'Amour recommended writers "shoot the sheriff on the first page" (meaning, present the problem.) He also gave another piece of advice appropriate here:

"Bring your main character on in action."

Exactly. And that advice is appropriate not only for adventure stories.

Do not have an opening scene with your main character laying in bed alone and thinking. Do not bring your character on sitting in an easy chair in a living room and thinking; or going for a walk and musing about life. Do not start your story with a minor character. Do not start your story with your main character's birth.

In the Dramatic Form, the beginning takes place during a moment of tension usually brought about by a change – change of circumstance such as leaving for someplace; arriving someplace, or someone else arriving or leaving.

If you take that advice and then introduce your main character in action, you may save yourself from having to take the advice of Chekhov to fold in two, and tear up the first half.

In addition, as the previous chapter points out, the opening paragraph of the opening scene must create for the reader the point of view; the "voice;" the mood; plus the fundamental job of making him want to know what is going to happen next, and in the words of Sean O'Faolain: "To strike the key-note at once!"

That's a tall order.

How many times will you have to rewrite your opening scene? I know how many times I would – at least a dozen; and then dozens of more polishes "getting the words right."

Put a Salamander In It

When I am introduced as a writer, I have always been surprised at the number of people who approach me later and say:

"I have three chapters of a novel written, but I just haven't had time to finish it."

They look at me expectantly, apparently hoping I will tell them how to find the time; or barring that, where to go in their novel, because I am quite sure it is not time that has stopped them, but the reaching of a dead end in their story.

Sculptor Benvenuto Cellini, in his autobiography, said that one day as a child sitting by the fireplace with his father, they both saw a salamander in the flames. Cellini said his father boxed his ears so that he wouldn't forget what he saw.

Edith Wharton, known for her short stories as well as her novels, explained:

This anecdote might serve as an apothegm for the writer of stories. If his first stroke be vivid and telling, the reader's attention will be instantly won. This leads to another point: It is useless to box your reader's ear unless you have a salamander to show him. The salamander stands for that fundamental significance that made the story worth telling.

In my view, if you have not determined a theme for your story and have not planned the plot all the way to the denouement (the salamander); your story will end up as simply an opening scene stuffed away in a drawer with no place to go as are, perhaps, millions of others.

It is the theme revealed in the denouement that gives your story its "fundamental significance" and makes it worth telling. So, don't box your reader's ears until you have a salamander in hand.

What They Say

'Get Black on White' used to be de Maupassant's advice – that's what I always do. I don't give a hoot what the writing's like. I write any sort of rubbish which will cover the main outlines of the story. Then I begin to see it. When I write, when I draft a story, I never think of writing nice sentences, I just write roughly what happened. I have to wait for the theme before I can do anything.

— Frank O'Connor

(Elsewhere, I have recommended you write a plot narrative and a one-sentence theme before starting. This is similar to, if not the same as, what O'Connor is saying.)

PART V

The Involvement

22 Is It True, or Did You Make It Up?

I have been asked the question in the title many times, both as a journalist and as a fiction writer, and I have never known to which of the two options I should admit – especially when my newspaper editor asked the question.

Where do stories come from? Does the stork bring them?

I know where some (if not all) stories come from. They come from the writer's own experience, such as those in the memoirs of Beryl Markham's *West With The Night,* or Norman Maclean's *A River Runs Through It.*

Maclean describes his book as "fictionalized autobiography." I think that's a description that could fit almost all stories – not just memoirs. We certainly have to draw upon our own perceptions and memory to tell any story, and our memory and perceptions are created from our experiences.

I recommend both the aforementioned books for study because they both contain wonderfully-told stories. Markham had an adventurous life about which she wrote glamorous stories, and Maclean had a rather ordinary life, about which he wrote adventurous stories.

Surely your life must fit somewhere between these two extremes.

To carry that idea a little further, Ernest Hemingway had an adventurous life and John Steinbeck had an ordinary life, but they both wrote perceptive and exciting stories.

In the case of Steinbeck most of his stories are set in California's Salinas Valley where he was born and raised. It is a fairly dull area which includes such places as "Cannery Row" in Monterey, at that time a dumpy small town on the coast where sardines were canned.

A story about Cannery Row could be seen by Californians as being about as exciting as Iowans would expect a story set in a meat packing plant in Ottumwa to be.

C. S. Forester, author of *The African Queen*, is one of Britain's leading historians. All of his books are set in the midst of historical events, including the above story which is set at the beginning of World War I. *Gone With the Wind* is set in the midst of the U.S. Civil War.

Steinbeck is a good subject to examine in trying to determine where stories come from – if it's not, indeed, the stork that brings them.

Most of his stories are set in what I've already described as a rather dull valley – *Of Mice and Men*, *East of Eden*, *The Red Pony*, *Cannery Row*, *Tortilla Flat*, *Sweet Thursday* to name a few. The characters are drawn from the types of people who live there.

These books illustrate one of the pieces of advice contained in every how-to book – write about what you know.

To further illustrate this point, Steinbeck's greatest book, *The Grapes of Wrath*, which brought him the Pulitzer Prize (and later, as part of his body of work, the Nobel Prize for Literature), was about the migrant workers who descended upon California after being forced from their midwest farms during the dust bowl years.

Steinbeck lived with the migrants, traveled with them, and picked fruit with them for a year before he considered writing this story which documented one of the great social tragedies of 20th Century America.

You might say Steinbeck was a journalist – that he was reporting on the tragedy. Is *The Grapes of Wrath* true, or did he make it up?

Steinbeck's writing also illustrates another source of stories – the hearing or reading of an anecdote.

The story *The Pearl* came about after he visited La Paz on the Baja Peninsula in Mexico. In a diary of that trip, Steinbeck said he heard an anecdote about a La Paz pearl fisherman who found "the pearl of the world." When the pearl buyers tried to cheat him out of it, he got so mad he threw it back in the ocean.

Of course, to this "incredible" story Steinbeck had to add characters, suspense, conflict, change, give it a theme and then cast it into the dramatic form – the same thing you have to do when you tell a story. You might read *The Pearl* to see how a master does it.

James Houston, whose description of "the master storyteller" led the chapter on scene writing, spent many years living in the Arctic. All his books are of this region and all are based upon stories he heard there.

He headed a three-day writer's workshop in Calgary, Canada, a few years ago, and he told the assembled writers that in the journal of Canadian explorer David Thompson, there is an account of Thompson's group coming across an Indian boy crawling in the woods high in the Rocky Mountains.

Upon questioning him, they learned the boy was blind, and the reason he crawled was to avoid falling down in the rough terrain. The boy had no relatives in the tribe to which he belonged, except a sister. The sister was married to a man who didn't want the boy, and so he lived in the mountains by himself, surviving on roots and plants which he could find and dig up. Occasionally his sister came and left skins for clothing and some food.

"I can't believe a Western Canadian writer has not made a story of this incident," Houston told the group of writers. "I can't do it because it's not my story . . . it's yours. What I know about is the Arctic."

Houston has this to say about his book, *White Dawn*:

Here is the first written account of the fate that befell the crew of a small whaleboat whose harpooner struck a whale that towed them far beyond return to their mother ship and into freezing fog and moving ice north of Hudson Bay, the very heart of the Eskimo world.

This saga is based on true events, related to me during the twelve years I lived in the Canadian eastern Arctic, roaming free in search of Eskimo art, and later serving as the first civil administrator of West Baffin Island.

So, you can see, *The Pearl* and *White Dawn* had the same seed — a "true" seed.

The following is a paraphrased paragraph from the back cover of *White Dawn*.

In the icy cold of the eastern Arctic, three survivors from a whaling misadventure are nursed back to life by a small Eskimo community and welcomed into its rhythms of hunting, fishing, feasting, and lovemaking. How they are received, what they learn, and what ultimately tragic changes they work on this highly developed yet isolated people give unforgettable power to this novel, which has become a classic portrayal of Eskimo life.

A reviewer from the San Francisco Examiner adds: "Delightful, gracefully written and damned informative. It proves that fiction can lend itself wonderfully to the passing on of a lode of anthropological lore."

What amazes me about this review is that the reviewer acts as though he had just discovered that one learns something by reading fiction.

I believe that someone who had read only fiction during his life would probably know more about the world he lives in and his relationship to it, than those who had read only textbooks.

In my opinion, most readers of fiction would be pretty disappointed if they didn't learn something after plunking down some cash for a book – at the very least something about the human condition. That is another reason why authors urge beginning writers to write about what they know.

A surprising number of fiction writers are historians. I've mentioned Forester, one of the leading authorities on the British Age of Empire; Margaret Mitchell was well-known as an expert on the U. S. Civil War before writing *Gone With the Wind*; Louis L'Amour reportedly had more than 1 000 books on America's Old West history in his personal library, many of the books rare editions, or one-of-a-kind; Dorothy Johnson wrote several Western history books including *The Bozeman Trail*, as did Marie Sandoz who wrote, in addition to her fiction, the books *Crazy Horse* and *Cheyenne Autumn*; America's greatest poet, Carl Sandburg, received the Pulitzer Prize for history for the first volume of his two-volume work on Abraham Lincoln.

Calgary playwright Sharon Pollock gets most of her stories from Canadian history – in most cases, the history we would like to forget.

Her *Komagata Maru* is the horrible story about Canadian authorities who, at the urging of the Canadian people, refused to allow a shipload of Sikhs to land in Vancouver. Although as Commonwealth subjects they had every legal right to immigrate, they were refused permission to land, thereby dooming them to starvation and death aboard the ship Komagata Maru.

At the same time, the Canadian parliament hurriedly passed a law – an unconstitutional law – to try to legalize their racist and inhuman action. A story best forgotten? Perhaps. In any case you won't find it in school history books. She, of course, added characters, suspense . . . Was her story true, or did she make it up?

Theodore Dreiser, in the classic *An American Tragedy*, took the facts from newspaper stories of his day of "the crime of the century." (This was before O.J.) He used every fact disclosed in the well-reported trial. Of course, he took those facts and added characters, suspense, conflict, change; organized them into a meaningful significance (theme); and put them into the dramatic form . . . all the elements you also have to add in order to make a story. Was his story true, or did he make it up?

A great many "creative" writers are or were journalists. Coming quickly to mind are Paul St. Pierre, from whom I have quoted extensively; Hemingway; Charles Dickens; Margaret Mitchell; Carl Sandburg; Dorothy Johnson. Journalists, of course, are writing history. (I put "creative" in quotes because, it seems to me, anyone filling that blank page with words is being creative.)

What if . . .

One can also come up with the seeds for stories by asking the question: "What if . . ."

Dorothy Johnson told me she got the idea for *The Hanging Tree* while watching a movie in New York City. Ms. Johnson explained she was a magazine editor there and lonesome for her home country, Montana. She attended two western movies on two successive nights, and both were about men lost in the desert.

"I thought . . . *What if there was a woman lost in the desert? . . .*" and the classic *The Hanging Tree* was born.

Other sources include starting from a theme, or from an incident, or as Eudora Welty says, "hearing a bird song." But no matter what the inspiration, you must add to it characters, suspense, conflict, theme, and you must cast it into the dramatic form.

Still Another Question

Shortly after publication of my memoir, *The Education of a Badlands Boy*, which contains about 40 stories, some of which go back to my pre-school years, a man I knew had read the book walked up to me. Without any preamble such as "I liked your book" or "I hated your book," he planted himself before me with legs wide apart, fists on hips, and said:

"How much did you embellish your stories?"

How does a story writer answer that?

I still haven't figured out how to answer: "Is it true, or did you make it up?"

Garrison Keillor of *Lake Wobegon* fame said his stories were "89 per cent true."

I wish I had said that.

Hemingway made clear in a number of interviews that his goal as a writer was to "write truly." It is also my goal . . . perhaps the goal of every writer.

But "truly" and "the truth" may be different things. One of the first concepts journalism students must learn is that they are not writing a list of facts. They are writing a story. And as Hayakawa's story definition states: *abstracting only the significant events and organizing them into a meaningful significance.*

I have already mentioned that "a life" does not make a story, and used the example of the life of Charles Lindbergh being composed of 50 percent living as a recluse and 10 percent dying of cancer.

But even if you were to make a story of the tiny dramatic part of Lindbergh's life, you would not write every part. You would skip the time spent going to the bathroom, shaving, sleeping, eating, arguing with his wife, reading, talking on the telephone, etc.

I remember watching the move "The Lone Eagle." I and the rest of the audience were all on the edge of our seats. Was Lindbergh going to make it across the Atlantic before the gasoline ran out, before he fell asleep, before the storm hit? Of course, we all knew that he did make it, but we readers and viewers are perfectly prepared to allow good story writers have their way with us. And a good story writer leaves out everything that is not significant to the story. Was "The Lone Eagle" true, or was it made up?

The problem is that what is "significant" to one person may be "insignificant" to another; that's why there are so many books about Lindbergh by different authors.

I always told my journalism students when they were going out to cover an event as a group that if any two of them came back with the same story they would both get an "F" and perhaps expelled from school for cheating.

As to the question asked

Did I, in covering an ev
the whole truth? Or did I al
significant events, and orga
significance – making a sto.

This generation, with its access to CNN and its co.
coverage of some events, may be the first to understand fully how
little of the truth there is in a few paragraphs of a newspaper news
story, or in a 20-second "bite" on TV news.

Garrison Keillor's 89 percent true? That's good !

Clearly, you can only write your truth. If you have had the
experience and have had the understanding of your experience,
perhaps you can write what will become to others their truth – part
of their experience.

It takes maturity to be a writer, which can come at a relatively
young age for some. There are no child prodigies in the story
writing field as there are in music or in mathematics.

Pulitzer Prize winning author Wallace Stegner described stories
as "inventions on a base of experience."

What They Say

*In one way and another I have used in my writings whatever
has happened to me in the course of my life. Sometimes an
experience I have had has served as a theme and I have
invented a series of incidents to illustrate it; more often I have
taken persons with whom I have been slightly or intimately
acquainted and used them as the foundation for characters of
my own invention. Fact and fiction are so intermingled in my
work I can hardly distinguish one from the other.*

– W. Somerset Maugham

For Ⲩ   *ɪg?*

The chapter title is a legitima. argue about the grammar. You c. young adults, for sophisticated reao. slick magazine or pulp magazine reao.

: might .ɪren, for .ɑers, or for

You could be writing for the vast audi. as classic westerns, science fiction, Harleq. mystery, or spy thrillers.

.ɡenre books such ɪˈ Gothic Romance,

Or you could be writing for another vast audience for "best sellers."

If you are a college professor you might even be writing to impress your fellow professors.

For whom are you writing? The question might be best addressed by asking another.

WHO ARE YOU?

I've known some pretty good writers who decided to "knock off a few Harlequins" with ego-smashing results. They should have suspected they couldn't write a Harlequin when they discovered they had to FORCE themselves to read some of them to get an idea of the formula. It's been said that half the women in North America are reading Harlequins, and the other half are writing them. (But not many of the latter are getting published.)

I've known a few beginners who plan to start out writing a literary story and set the literary world on its ear, even though they read only Harlequins and have never heard of the *Saturday Review of Literature.*

I've read advice by quite a few authors to "write what you like to read." It makes sense to me, and I pass it on.

For whom are you writing? You must be writing for a reader – not for yourself – but that reader, perhaps, is someone just like you.

Write what you know. Write what you like to read.

Two gems of advice, although one can find successful writers who demonstrate exceptions to both.

However, the principles of story writing remain the same in all cases. The elements and the structure of the story and the fundamentals of vivid writing do not change regardless of for whom you are writing. A "formula," as in a Harlequin, is placed ON the story form. First, you must organize a good story, using the dramatic form and all the elements, and second, you put it into the formula.

Who-is-the-audience does make one difference, however.

Although I have insisted that in your scenes you write description, action and dialogue – little explanation, or little thinking – the writing for some audiences does contain explanation and thinking. This is the writing for Harlequin readers, for true confession readers, for classic westerns and other genres. Nevertheless, I urge that you "show," not "tell," because beginning writers, in my experience, can already tell a story. They need to learn how to "show" it.

I will illustrate with examples of the writing in two main groups – genre writers and serious writers – taken from *Language in Thought and Action*, by S. I. Hayakawa.

From a True Confession:

Telling Mrs. Peters and Mrs. Jenks, watching grief engulf them, was nightmare enough, but telling Edie was worst of all. She just stood there in frozen silence, her eyes wide with horror and disbelief, her face getting whiter and whiter.

"I did everything possible to save them!" I cried. "it was an accident – an unpreventable accident!"

But Edie's eyes were bitterly accusing as she choked, "Accident! If you hadn't insisted on taking them, there would have been no accident!" Tears streamed down her ravaged face and her voice rose hysterically, "I never want to see you again as long as I live! You – you murderer!" she screamed.

I stared at her for what seemed a lifetime of horror before I turned and fled, a million shrieking demons screaming in my ear, She's right! You're a murderer! Murderer!

Doesn't leave much room for our imagination, does it? Our involvement is unnecessary.

I have watched people on the bus reading a genre-type paperback. They read a bit. Stare out the window. Read a bit. Watch the other passengers. Read a bit. As you can see from the above example, the author does not require anything from the reader. The book is simply chewing gum for the mind. Now, the final scene of Hemingway's *A Farewell to Arms*:

I went into the room and stayed with Catherine until she died. She was unconscious all the time, and it did not take her very long to die.

Outside the room, in the hall, I spoke to the doctor, "Is there anything I can do tonight?"

"No, there is nothing to do. Can I take you to your hotel? "

"No, thank you. I am going to stay here a while."

"I know there is nothing to say. I cannot tell you –"

"No," I said. "there's nothing to say."

"Goodnight," he said. "I cannot take you to your hotel?"

"No, thank you."

"It was the only thing to do," he said. "the operation proved –"

"I do not want to talk about it," I said.

"I would like to take you to your hotel."

"No, thank you."

He went down the hall. I went to the door of the room.

"You can't come in now," one of the nurses said.

"Yes I can," I said.

"You can't come in yet."

"You get out," I said. "The other one too."

But after I had got them out and shut the door and turned off the light it wasn't any good. It was like saying goodby to a statue. After a while I went out and left the hospital and walked back to the hotel in the rain.

As you can see, Hemingway simply reported what happened and what was said. We must fill in the thoughts and emotions which we can readily do having come to know, and to become involved with the character during the course of reading the book.

An interviewer asked Hemingway if he did much rewriting. "Depends," said Hemingway, probably with tongue in cheek: "I rewrote the final scene in *A Farewell to Arms* 29 times."

The interviewer asked: "What was the problem?"

Hemingway explained: "Getting the words right."

Another important difference between the writers of the above examples: Hemingway has explained, (as have other authors) that his goal was to write "truly." He would not write "*a million shrieking devils were screaming in my ear.*"

A million is quite a few devils. Even for a lifetime of horror.

What They Say

I don't mean anything flamboyant by the phrase 'telling the truth.' I don't mean exposing anything. By truth I mean accuracy – it is largely a matter of style. It is my duty to society not to write: 'I stood above a bottomless gulf' or 'going downstairs, I got into a taxi,' because these statements are untrue. My characters must not go white in the face or tremble like leaves, not because these phrases are clichés, but because they are untrue . . . every time a phrase like one of these passes into the mind uncriticized, it muddies the stream of thought.

– Graham Greene

24 How to Live More Than One Life

I have indicated this is not a literature book. Even though I love literature and love discussing it, I do not think you can WRITE literature. You can only write a story.

However, it may happen the story you write will be so "true" that generations of readers will be able to relate to it, and for a time, live a life other than their own. In other words, your story could <u>become</u> literature.

As Ernest Hemingway wrote:

A writer's problem does not change. He himself changes and the world he lives in changes, but the problem remains the same. It is always how to write truly and, having found what is true, to project it in such a way that it becomes a part of the experience of the person who reads it.

It might be useful to your sense of purpose, therefore, to understand the role of literature in our lives.

S. I. Hayakawa, in his famous book *Language in Thought and Action*, has a chapter titled The Language of Affective Communication. (Note it is "affective" not "effective.") He explains literature communicates feelings, rather than facts. "An author may write an entire book simply to communicate the proposition that 'Life is Tragic.' – not by TELLING us so, but by SHOWING us it is so through a whole series of experiences by the characters."

Hayakawa writes:

In a very real sense, then, people who have read good literature have lived more than people who cannot or will not read. To have read Gulliver's Travels is to have had the experience, with Jonathan Swift, of turning sick to one's stomach at the conduct of the human race; to read Huckleberry Finn is to feel what it is like to drift down the Mississippi River on a raft; to have read Byron is to have suffered with him his rebellions and neuroses and to have enjoyed with him his nose-thumbing at society; to have read Native Son *is to know how it felt to be frustrated in the particular way in which many Blacks in Chicago were frustrated. This is the great task affective communication performs; it enables us to feel how others felt about life, even if they lived thousands of miles away and centuries ago. It is not true that we have only one life to live; if we can read, we can live as many more lives and as many kinds of lives as we wish.*

To bring this thought up to date . . . we are never going to know what it feels like to be in a spaceship circling the earth until we send up a poet, for poetry is the highest form of *affective* writing. If you ask one of the engineer-type astronauts what it is like up there, he says: "Fantastic, wonderful, incredible." In other words, adjectives; and I've already pointed out how ineffective adjectives are in communicating feelings.

Hayakawa goes on to explain:

In the enjoyment of a work of literary art – a novel, a play, a movie – we find our deepest enjoyment when the leading characters in the story to some degree symbolize ourselves. Jessie Jenkins at the movie watching Elizabeth Taylor being kissed by a handsome man, sighs contentedly as if she herself were being kissed – and symbolically she is. Or when Kirk Douglas fights a villain, millions of men in the audience clench their fists as if they were doing the fighting – and symbolically they are.

However, he points out, there is a great gulf between actual experience and symbolic experience, because real life is chaotic.

Our life, as he explains, even at the moment we may be having a great love affair, is interrupted with such things as an argument with our boss, having to prepare a meal, going to see the doctor about our fallen arches, hurrying to the post office to get some stamps before it closes. So much for our glorious romance.

Hayakawa points out: "Abstracting only the significant events and organizing them into a meaningful significance, constitutes the storyteller's art."

He goes on to explain that plot, character, climax, denouement and all the other aspects of story structure are for one purpose: to have a desired impact on the reader."

Consequently, that "desired impact" is what we call the "theme." And as pointed out elsewhere, your story must have a theme, and you must understand it clearly enough so you can write it into one sentence. Without a theme – a "desired impact" – why do the things in your story happen? If you are simply writing "life" – scattering happenings through your story, and recording pointless dialogue – you are going to lose us readers, because we are already living chaotic lives. We want to read about lives that lead to something.

Hayakawa says immature readers insist all the stories they read have a happy ending. They go though their real lives trying to avoid unpleasantness, and they are not about to face it symbolically in a story.

Mature readers, on the other hand, steadily increase the depth and range of their symbolic experiences. They are prepared to symbolically experience murder, guilt, religious exaltation, bankruptcy, etc.

For example, in Conrad's *Lord Jim* the "hero" is living with the knowledge that he is a coward and his cowardice could have doomed hundreds of men to death. Does he win out over the impact of this knowledge, or is he defeated by it? Read on . . .

Hayakawa explains the willingness to read about "unpleasant" experiences gives mature readers a widening consciousness of the world and of other lives, and gives them "more accurate pictures" of human character and behavior under many different conditions and in different times.

These insights, then, give us sympathy with our fellow human beings everywhere, and when the lives of other people, of whatever time and place, are examined in this way, "we discover to our amazement that they are all people." He adds that it is this discovery which is the basis of all *civilized* human relationships.

According to Hayakawa, the extent that these relationships break down in our own personal lives, or our own society, shows the extent that we have not made this discovery – the discovery that all people, of whatever time and place, are people – German, Russian, Somalian, Jew, Canadian, Catholic, Blacks, Whites, Indians, rich and poor, our boss, our fellow worker. He claims literature is one of the most important instruments for bringing about this discovery and "civilizing" our relationships.

He explains that science enables us to exchange INFORMATION. Literature enables us to exchange FEELINGS and thereby understand each other – "to cease being brutishly suspicious of each other and to realize the profound community that exists between us and our fellow men."

I think you will agree that Hayakawa's view of literature (perhaps your ultimate goal in writing) is worth thinking about.

When he wrote about "immature" readers, he used the word "insist." That is, he didn't say one is immature if they read Harlequin romances or classic Westerns where the problems and solutions are simple and inevitable, the heroes and villains easily distinguishable, the endings always happy. He said if one *insists* on reading *only* such books they are immature readers, and their relationships with other people may also be on the same black and white, good and evil basis.

25 *The Essential Oneness*

Many young people when they go to university are, for the first time, taught to think. I know that was the case for me.

Even though I had become a prodigious reader by the age of five, I had never learned to analyze what I read – that is, to question. I was simply a sponge. Then to learn in university that it was perfectly all right to question all that I had read, all that I had been taught, all that my parents believed in, was pretty heady stuff.

I remember coming home on holidays and telling my father how he should run his newspaper; telling my mother all the things she thought were important were actually nonsense.

It embarrasses me now to remember.

However, my affliction was a common one. So common there is a name for it – "Sophomoric." And it has given rise to bumper stickers such as: "Hire a Student While They Still Know Everything."

Fortunately it has a cure – time. Most students grow out of it, and while each new generation refuses to adopt all of the previous generation's values, it adopts enough of the them to furnish society with continuity. (Except, perhaps, the 1960s generation of rebels.)

This long introduction leads to a discussion of "literature," specifically a university course called "Great Books" where undergraduates read a "Great Book" and then sit around and discuss it without an instructor leading them.

This free-wheeling discussion leads students to realize there are many ways to interpret a story; many ways to look at life; many ways to live life. And it leads them to question everything.

The course was so successful in getting students to think that educators decided it would be a good idea to extend it to high school.

What a disaster!

It wasn't that the course didn't teach the high school students to think. The problem was that it did. To think is to question, and educators discovered that was the last thing parents and teachers wanted.

They gave lip service to the idea that Johnny and Jane should be taught to think . . . but not to question their parents or teachers. ("Why? Because I said so, that's why!") In communities where the course was introduced there developed mass protests of parents and teachers, and the noble experiment was quickly dropped.

When we read great books, when we analyze and question, when we live symbolically other lives in other times, we discover we are, at our core, all human beings with the same feelings despite the realization that different generations and different cultures have different values and different ways of viewing life.

I think you should have this in your mind when you sit down and write. You should consider that someone, or perhaps generations of someone will discover in your story, written from your unique perspective, the essential oneness of humanity.

So, don't stick up your nose at "story writing."

According to Forster: "Oh dear yes. You must tell a story. And I wish it were not so. I wish it were music, or perception of truth, not this low atavistic form."

You can write your "perception of truth" in an essay, or in a sermon, or you can shout it from a soapbox. But if you want to affect someone – touch their emotions – you must put it in the form of a story.

The Bible, as I've pointed out, is chock full of stories, all pointing to what Christians think of as great truths. It is argued that all the story lines are in the Bible.

Those from the East would probably argue that all stories have their roots in the Koran, or in the stories told by Confucius. And we can understand their view, for as readers of literature, we have discovered there is no fundamental difference in humanness between *us* and *them*.

Stories are the way universal truths that affect us are communicated – East and West.

What They Say

Every man who knows how to read has it in his power to magnify himself, to multiply the ways in which he exists, to make his life full, significant and interesting.

— Aldous Huxley

When you re-read a classic you do not see more in the book than you did before; you see more in YOU than was there before.

— Clifton Fadiman

Those whom books will hurt will not be proof against events. If some books are deemed more baneful and their sale forbid, how, then with deadlier facts, not dreams of doting men? Events, not books, should be forbid.

— Herman Melville

The man who does not read good books has no advantage over the man who can't read them.

— Mark Twain

Why do people always expect authors to answer questions? I am an author because I want to ASK questions. If I had the answers I would be a politician.

— Eugene Ionesco

26 *The Secret Places of the Soul . . .*

The following is a pearl discovered in what I consider to be a sea of mud in James Joyce's *Ulysses,* written in Stream of Consciousness style:

. . . and then I asked him with my eyes to ask again yes

and then he asked me would I yes . . .

and first I put my arms around him yes

and drew him down to me so he could feel my breasts all perfume yes

and his heart was going like mad

and yes I said yes I will yes.

Somewhat more affective than if the author had simply written: "Then she said, 'yes'."

Stream of consciousness was a writing fad of the '20s through the '40s which was intended to be a representation of the rambling chaos of our thoughts. Used carefully and in a poetic fashion, such as in the example above, it was, and is, affective.

In my view, stream of consciousness works when used with caution – when strong emotion is to be conveyed such as at the denouement or at other key points of change in a story.

A writer must be aware of pace in the story, and cannot expect the reader to stay at a high level of tension or emotion throughout. The problem with Joyce and other authors who first experimented with stream of consciousness is that they used the technique throughout, and in the end the only emotions their readers felt were confusion and boredom.

The following soliloquy in *The Grapes of Wrath* is the denouement and comes just where one would expect it in the dramatic form – a few pages before the end of the next-to-last chapter.

The speech by Tom — which is essentially stream of consciousness as Tom gropes in his mind — shows what one reviewer said the whole book was about: ". . . the survival of human dignity and spirit under the most desperate conditions."

Tom is talking to his mother here in his hideout where he had gone after his friend, Casey, while protesting against injustice, was killed by a deputy. Tom had in turn killed the deputy. Tom is telling his mother that he has to leave, and that he will carry on Casey's work.

They sat silent in the coalblack cave of vines. Ma said, "How'm I gonna know 'bout you? They might kill ya an' I wouldn' know. They might hurt ya. How'm I gonna know?"

Tom laughed uneasily. "Well, maybe like Casey says, a fella ain't got a soul of his own, but on'y a piece of a big one – an' then –"

"Then what, Tom?"

"Then it don' matter. Then I'll be all aroun' in the dark. I'll be ever'where – wherever you look. Wherever they's a fight so hungry people can eat, I'll be there. Wherever they's a cop beatin' up a guy, I'll be there. If Casey knowed, why, I'll be in the way guys laugh when they're hungry an' they know supper's ready. An' when our folks eat the stuff they raise an' live in the houses they build – why, I'll be there."

This speech, then, is the resolution, the point, the change. At this lowest point in the Joad family's fight for survival when all seems to be lost, we readers know, after this soliloquy, that the Joad family will survive, and after some more vicissitudes, will prosper much like the turtle which made it across the road, planted a seed, and continued on, although "his yellow toe nails slipped a fraction in the dust." (See Appendix.)

The soliloquy was given by Henry Fonda in the movie and I doubt if there was a dry eye in the house.

The power of this soliloquy lies in what is said, of course, but also in the rhythm very much like the rhythm of the stream of consciousness example from Joyce.

As Plato said centuries ago: "Music and rhythm find their way into the secret places of the soul."

I gather that Steinbeck was saying in *The Grapes of Wrath* the same thing that Anne Frank wrote in her diary when she was 13 after three years of hiding in a tiny attic room from the Nazis: "Despite everything, I still believe people are good at heart."

Elsewhere I have advised writers not to have their characters making speeches.

I stick by that advice. But there are exceptions. The soliloquy by Tom, for example. However, wouldn't it have been awful if Steinbeck had his characters giving speeches every time they opened their mouths?

I have also advised writers not to have their characters talk like English professors. Certainly, Tom does not. Clearly a character does not have to talk like an English professor in order to say something profound and moving.

I have never had anywhere near the terrible experiences of the Joad family or Anne Frank, but I must confess that I do not believe that people are "good at heart," especially not the Nazis who eventually hunted down and killed Anne Frank because she was a Jew, or the fruit growers in California who took advantage of the desperate circumstances of the migrant workers and paid them starvation wages.

Nevertheless, we writers must try to see what is in the hearts of the characters we create and to communicate it, not entirely with words, but with music and rhythm to touch the reader's soul.

Norman Maclean wrote in the acknowledgments to *A River Runs Through It*, that he had shown the first part of his manuscript to a poet friend who advised him to put a little poetry in it to express his love for the land.

And he did.

In my view, he put in just the right amount. You might read the book and see what you think.

Here is what Maclean wrote in one story telling of the early days of the U.S. Forest Service when a young boy (Norman Maclean) was sent to the top of a mountain with nothing but a pup tent, a telephone and an alidade to spot lightning strikes and watch for fires:

But what I remember best is crawling out of the tent on summer nights when on high mountains autumn is always approaching. To a boy, it is something new and beautiful to piss among the stars. Not under the stars but among them. Even at night great winds seem always to blow on great mountains, and tops of trees bend, but, as the boy stands there with nothing to do but to watch, seemingly the sky itself bends and the stars blow down through the trees until the Milky Way becomes lost in some distant forest. As the cosmos brushes by the boy and disappears among the trees, the sky is continually replenished with stars. There would be stars enough to brush by him all night, but by now the boy is getting cold.

Then the shivering organic speck of steam itself disappears.

Rhythm and music . . .

Keep in mind the readers do not only want their mind titillated, wondering what is going to happen next. Your story must also touch the secret places of the reader's soul.

Odds and ENDS

Some of the quotes from authors in this book are taken from *The Writer's Quote Book*, edited by James Charlton. Others are taken from my own files gleaned from years of obsessive reading.

In reading biographies, autobiographies and memoirs of authors, I have noticed that a great many of them, in addition to being wide readers, were also addicted to keeping journals.

For the young person hopeful of becoming an author, I recommend this practice, although I never kept a journal as a young man. My only goal was to be a "good reporter." I was in love with the day-to-dayness of the news – and of life.

Later, when I became, as they say, no longer young, I started keeping extensive files. With the advent of the computer age, it is now much easier than the keeping of journals of yesteryear – and just as useful.

James Joyce wrote to a young nephew who had asked for some advice on how to prepare himself to become a writer: "Try to become the kind of person on whom nothing is lost."

In my view, even imagination is rooted in experience and everything you will ever write will come from your experience. Much of that experience will come from the living of other lives in the pages of literature.

Author Elizabeth Bowen explains:

Though not all reading children grow up to be writers, I take it that most creative writers must in their day have been reading children.

All through creative writing must run a sense of the dishonest and of debt. In fact, is there such a thing, any more, as creative writing? The imagination, which may appear to bear such individual fruit, is rooted in a compost of forgotten books.

Almost no experience can be couched as wholly my own – did I live through that, or was I told that it happened, or did I read it? When I write I am re-creating what was created for me. I may see, for instance, a road running uphill, a skyline, a figure

coming slowly over the hill – the approach of the figure is
momentous, accompanied by fear or rapture. But who and how
is this? Am I sure this is not a figure out of a book?

As I mentioned elsewhere, in the field of writing there are no child prodigies. It takes experience, of one kind or another, to have something to say.

What They Say

Following are some tid-bits of vivid description I have come across. You won't find any commonplaces or clichés here:

From Sybille Bedford in *The Sudden View* set in Mexico, published in 1953 (also published as *A Visit to Don Octavio.*): A Mexican storm . . .

Since then I have remembered that evening – how, just before it grew dark, the tattered banana trees writhed like gigantic seaweed in the wind, and the cold rain hissed from the spouts on the roof in graceful, crystal tubes . . .

. . . The sickening smell of tequila – raw alcohol with an underwiff of festering sweetness as though chrysanthemums had rotted in gin . . .

The Mexican Santo Thomas wine she describes as tasting like "cheap ink dosed with industrial alcohol, as harsh on the tongue as a carrot-grater."

A tropical nightfall ". . . Darkness descends with a sudden extinguishing sweep like the cover on the canary's cage."

A description of Venice, Italy after a rain, by Gustave Flaubert: ". . . wobbling in a thousand fresh-water reflections, cool as jelly."

Captain Joshua Slocum setting out on the first single-handed circumnavigation of the globe in his boat, "Spray," wrote in his journal:

The day was perfect, the sunlight clear and strong. Every particle of water thrown into the air became a gem and the "Spray," bounding ahead, snatched necklace after necklace from the sea, and as often threw them away.

Here are two vivid character descriptions:

Author Evelyn Waugh has a loathsome character in each of his books, and he usually names the character with some variation of "Cruttwell." The original Cruttwell was the dean of Hertford College, Oxford, described thusly: "He was tall, almost loutish, with the face of a petulant baby. He smoked a pipe which was usually attached to his blubber lips by a thread of slime."

From John Steinbeck's play, *The Moon is Down*:

Beside the fireplace old Doctor Winter sat, bearded and simple and benign, historian and physician to the town. He watched in amazement while his thumbs rolled over and over on his lap. Doctor Winter was a man so simple that only a profound man would know him as profound.

Barbara Tuchman, writing in *Guns of August*, a history of the start of World War I: "A sudden shiver of sabers glittered in the sun as the cavalry came to attention."

And her description of Count Alfred von Schlieffen, chief strategist for Germany's preparation for World War I and former chief of the General Staff:

Of the two classes of Prussian officer, the bullnecked and the wasp-waisted, he belonged to the second. Monocled and effete in appearance, cold and distant in manner, he concentrated with such single-mindedness on his profession that when an aide, at the end of an all-night staff ride in East Prussia, pointed out to him the beauty of the river Pregel sparkling in the rising sun, the General gave a brief, hard look and replied, "An unimportant obstacle."

(Notice how she put the character "in action" to support her description of him.)

These vivid writing examples come from travelogues, from history, from memoirs and from a play. As I've pointed out, there are no KINDS of writing such as fiction or non-fiction, there is only "Good Writing," "Mediocre Writing" and "Awful Writing."

Epilogue

Story telling is an old and honourable trade. The first stories were told around camp fires and the last will be told there too. They were told for people seeking to entertain themselves by examining the almost limitless varieties of the human animal. A story made some sort of order of men's affairs, but not too much. After all, luck arranges much of what we do and forces called fate, destiny or the devil do their share too. Most men who tell stories do not pretend to excessive understanding of what happens in them.

– Paul St. Pierre

APPENDIX

Excerpts from the Masters

What They Say

My belief is that nobody can be taught anything, that one must learn. I would say if I had a class of young people that wanted to write, I would make available to them everything that was ever written, with no distinction of time, period, style, but everything. Anyone who wants to write must read everything, trash, the best, the worst, everything, because he will never know when he will find something he can need and he will use because any writer is a thief and a robber. He will steal from any source, and he must read, should read, everything.

. . . It takes complete freedom of spirit to be the writer. He's got to make his own mistakes, he's got to learn, himself. I don't think you can teach him. He's got to have a desire to learn, the patience to learn and an infinite capacity to experiment, to make mistakes, to throw the mistakes away and try again.

— William Faulkner

(My opening statement to my writing classes is: "I'm not going to teach you anything. I'm simply going to give you the opportunity to learn.")

Immature artists imitate. Mature artists steal.

— Lionel Trilling

(Steal ideas, concepts, principles, techniques. As I wrote in the Introduction: Story writing, like the wheel, doesn't need to be reinvented. But don't steal published expressions and use them as your own — that's a violation of copyright laws. There's a name for it . . . plagiarism.)

Introduction to Appendix

To enable your reading and writing to be most beneficial to your goals, I believe you must TRY to write for a reader, and you must TRY to read as a writer reads.

Our audience reads, for the most part, to become emotionally involved with the characters in the story, and to find out what happens next.

We students of writing must read – learn to read – analytically, trying to discover how the masters accomplished their goal of involving the reader.

Therefore, I have included an appendix. I expect you to read the excerpts, getting yourself emotionally involved and curious about what happens next, as the master intended. Then, I expect you to re-read the excerpt, examining the writing analytically. I will help you by suggesting what you should look for, using the "nuts and bolts" I have described in the previous chapters.

In the end, I expect you to apply the analysis. In my view, the extent to which you learn to analyze your reading will depend on the extent to which your reading helps your writing. And to the extent you learn to apply the analyses to your writing will depend on the extent your writing develops.

Vivid Description

From *The Grapes of Wrath* – by John Steinbeck

This piece of writing, considered one of the classics in literature, leads off many anthologies. It is a transitional chapter (chapter 3) and constitutes a parable foreshadowing what happens to the Joad family when they travel to California as refugees from the southwestern dustbowl.

Strength of this scene comes from strong verbs, sensual details and metaphor for vividness and realness and parallelism and repetition for rhythm and emotion. Your assignment is to highlight all the strong verbs and metaphors and to note the parallelism and repetition (rhythm). Remember, I am using metaphor in its broad sense which includes such figures of speech as personification and simile. The first two paragraphs are partially done for you.

The Turtle

The concrete highway **was edged** with a mat of tangled, broken, dry grass, and the grass heads **were heavy** with oat beards to **catch** on a dog's coat, and foxtails to **tangle** in a horse's fetlocks, and clover burrs to **fasten** in sheep's wool; sleeping life **waiting** to be spread and dispersed, every seed **armed** with an appliance of dispersal, twisting darts and parachutes for the wind, little spears and balls of tiny thorns, and all **waiting** for animals and for the wind, for a man's trouser cuff or the hem of a woman's skirt, all **passive** but **armed** with appliances of activity, still, but each **possessed** of the anlage of movement.

The sun **lay** on the grass and warmed it, and in the shade under the grass the insects **moved**, ants and ant lions to **set** traps for them, grasshoppers to **jump** into the air and **flick** their yellow wings for a second, sow bugs like **little armadillos, plodding restlessly on many tender feet**. And over the grass at the roadside a land turtle **crawled**, turning aside for nothing, **dragging** his high-domed shell over the grass. His hard legs and yellow-nailed feet **threshed** slowly through the grass, not really walking, but boosting and dragging his shell along. The barley beards **slid** off his shell, and the clover burrs **fell** on him and **rolled** to the ground. His horny beak was partly open, and his **fierce,**

humorous eyes, under **brows like fingernails**, stared straight ahead. He came over the grass leaving a beaten trail behind him, and the hill, which was the highway embankment, reared up ahead of him.

For a moment he stopped, his head held high. He blinked and looked up and down. At last he started to climb the embankment. Front clawed feet reached forward but did not touch. The hind feet kicked his shell along, and it scraped on the grass, and on the gravel. As the embankment grew steeper and steeper, the more frantic were the efforts of the land turtle. Pushing hind legs strained and slipped, boosting the shell along, and the horny head protruded as far as the neck could stretch. Little by little the shell slid up the embankment until at last a parapet cut straight across its line of march, the shoulder of the road, a concrete wall four inches high. As though they worked independently the hind legs pushed the shell against the wall. The head upraised and peered over the wall to the broad plain of cement. Now the hands, braced on top of the wall, strained and lifted, and the shell came slowly up and rested its front end on the wall. For a moment the turtle rested. A red ant ran into the shell, into the soft skin inside the shell, and suddenly head and legs snapped in, and the armored tail clamped in sideways. The red ant was crushed between body and legs. And one head of wild oats was clamped into the shell by a front leg. For a long moment the turtle lay still, and then the neck crept out and the old humorous frowning eyes looked about and the legs and tail came out. The back legs went to work, straining like elephant legs and the shell tipped to an angle so that the front legs could not reach the level cement plain. But higher and higher the hind legs boosted it, until at last the center of balance was reached, the front tipped down, the front legs scratched at the pavement, and it was up. But the head of wild oats was held by its stem around the front legs.

Now the going was easy, and all the legs worked, and the shell boosted along, waggling from side to side. A sedan driven by a forty year old woman approached. She saw the turtle and swung to the right, off the highway, and wheels screamed and a cloud of dust boiled up. Two wheels lifted for a moment and then settled. The car skidded back onto the road, and went on, but more slowly. The turtle had jerked into its shell, but now it hurried on, for the highway was burning hot.

And now a light truck approached, and as it came near, the driver saw the turtle and swerved to hit it. His front wheel struck the edge of the shell, flipped the turtle like a tiddlywink, spun it like a coin, and rolled it off the highway. The truck went back to its course along the right side. Lying on its back, the turtle was tight in its shell for a long time. But at last its legs waved in the air, reaching for something to pull it over. Its front foot caught a piece of quartz and little by little the shell pulled over and flopped upright. The wild oat head fell out and three of the spearhead seeds stuck in the ground. And as the turtle crawled on down the embankment, its shell dragged dirt over the seeds. The turtle entered a dust road and jerked itself along, drawing a wavy shallow trench in the dust with its shell. The old humorous eyes looked ahead, and the horny beak opened a little. His yellow toe nails slipped a fraction in the dust.

In addition to all the elements of vivid writing that I have mentioned and that you have marked, the great power of this piece . . . its ability to get you, the reader, involved – lies in its incredible wealth of details and in its rhythms. These details – the "little particulars" – cause you to "see it," "feel it," "smell it" and make it real. You are there.

Imagination, that quality it is said that all writers must have, may lie here. It is the ability to see – to dredge up from the recesses of your memory – these details. It is not so much imagination that organizes a story, but imagination that visualizes details. One could picture Steinbeck crawling after a turtle with his notebook held in his teeth, but that's not the way it is done. No, Steinbeck most certainly "imagined" this scene while seated at his writing desk.

To write this, Steinbeck must have seen a land turtle crawling across a field at sometime; must have seen a road, must have seen enough of human nature to understand that some people would go out of their way to try and kill a turtle, and some people would almost kill themselves to avoid killing a turtle – as there are people who would go out of their way to hurt others and people who would go out of their way to help others. And, finally, he must have had the storytelling craft to organize the events happening to the turtle that would precisely parallel the events that would happen to the Joad family on its way to California.

The rest, as they say, is imagination, the little particulars – *yellow-nailed feet . . . boosting and dragging his shell along,* **and** *. . . the horny head protruded as far as the neck could stretch* **and** *. . . the going was easy . . . the shell boosted along, waggling from side to side, old humorous frowning eyes looked about* **and . . .**

entered a dusty road and jerked itself along, drawing a wavy shallow trench in the dust with its shell . . . a piece of quartz . . . a wild oat head and, finally: *His yellow toe nails slipped a fraction in the dust*. Note the turtle has been given human characteristics.

I hope it is clear from this scene, and from your efforts on scenes, that writing is perspiration not inspiration. This scene did not come effortlessly off the top of Steinbeck's head.

As author Gene Fowler said: "Writing is easy; all you do is sit in front of a blank sheet of paper until the drops of blood form on your forehead."

To write your scene, then, remember, imagine and bleed. Fill it with visual details and use the other senses as well. You may overwrite at first, but that's okay. It's much easier to take out than to put in. And again, don't write it perfectly. The only reason to write something down is so that it can be changed.

Make sure you have a tourniquet handy.

As Steinbeck explains in his prologue to *Sweet Thursday*, this is "hooptedoodle" – singing a song with language – and should be placed separately or at the beginning so as not to interfere with the story. He took his own advice. This short chapter of hooptedoodle is one of several in *The Grapes of Wrath*, all separate so readers can skip them if they wish.

Nevertheless, the elements of scene writing, intensified here to an extreme degree, while valid in your scene writing, must be used judiciously so as not to interfere with the story, the what-happens-next.

Vivid Scene Writing

From *Grizzly Country* – By Andy Russell

When I was growing up in South Dakota and reading everything I could get my hands on, I introduced myself to Andy Russell who, it seemed, had a story in every monthly outdoor magazine then published. He immediately became my hero. As I spent much of my time alone wandering over the prairies and Badlands of South Dakota, I day-dreamed myself as Andy Russell. I led pack trips into the wild Rocky Mountains of Canada, and guided a tenderfoot hunter to a world record elk, just like Andy.

So, it was a great thrill to me when I moved to Russell's home province of Alberta, and then learned he lived just a few miles from Calgary in Millarville. I have since met him several times, and he is everything I imagined him to be. I've read some of his recent works, and it's easy to see why I was captured and enraptured by his stories when I was a boy, because Russell is a master storyteller.

As I write this, Russell, now in his late 70s, writes every day, and continues to lead pack trips into the mountains and to take a leadership role in conservation. He is also the writer-in-residence at Lethbridge College. I have had him as a guest talking to my writing students, and he talks just as good a story as he writes.

Over lunch one day he told me about an assignment he had recently received from a magazine editor in New York City. The editor, apparently having read one of his wilderness stories, wrote an outline of an article he wanted Russell to do for him. In the letter, he had folded up a few sheets of blank paper, apparently imagining Russell sitting in a log cabin in the wilds of Canada with a stub of a pencil and possibly out of writing paper.

Andy took a sip of coffee, scratched his head and grinned at me:

"I sent him back his paper, and explained in my letter that it wouldn't fit in my computer." Andy was still chuckling when we left the coffee shop.

While Andy Russell plays and looks the part of the simple mountain man, believe me, he is not.

Here is his description of his backyard in his book, *Grizzly Country*. I should point out that it is also my backyard and could be, after reading this, yours.

You will notice that his vividness comes from the principles of scene writing I have been trying to impress upon you – strong

verbs, metaphors and details using all the senses. Also note description of the setting is incorporated into the action, and the main character (the grizzly) is brought on stage in action.

It was very early in the morning in mid-June. The stars were gone, except Venus, and night shadows lingered restively in the deeper folds among the hills and mountains. The air was cool and still, smelling of new grass, wild geraniums, and the golden blooms of Indian turnip, where the prairies sweep in close before soaring up to the saw-toothed eagle aeries along the sky.

The horse carried his head low, threading the winding trail at a fast running walk on a loose rein. Having bucked the kinks out of his frame and mine back at the corral gate a half hour earlier, he was now tending to business, his ears working to pick up the bells of the pack string scheduled to leave on the first trip of the season across the Rockies to the wilds of the Flathead River in British Columbia. He did no more than cock an ear at four big mule deer bucks, their stubs of new antlers sheathed in velvet, bounding up out of a draw in the long springy leaps so typical of their kind. When I reined him after them to the top of a lookout butte not far from Indian Springs, the red sun was just breaking over the rim of the plains to the east. On the crest the horse stopped of his own free will. We stood motionless, facing the sun with only a light zephyr of wind fingering his mane and the fringes of my buckskin jacket, as we watched the new day being born.

This is something of nature's witchery, when the night goes and the day comes to the living world. Nothing matches the back of a good horse as a place to watch it. No other place but here at the foot of the Rockies, where the prairies and the mountains meet, can its awesome and beautiful display be seen and felt so well. Only on a June morning, between the last of spring and the first of summer, does it impart such a feeling of sudden-bursting life. Here the Rockies are its great backdrop, a timber-topped ridge winging it to the north and the sprawling peaks of the Great Lewis Overthrust walling it off to the south. Mountain meadows, lakes, and ageless stone couple into solid magnificence. It is a marriage of light and life, a promise and a fulfillment of that promise. While the mountains light up at first sun in deep rose, swiftly changing to gold, and all shot through with deep purple shadow, it is as though the whole universe pauses for a long, heart-stretching moment, locked in a spell of deep wonder.

Not a sound broke the stillness that morning. The horse and I stood waiting, breathless. Then he gave a long sigh; the saddle creaked under me, and a spur rowel jingled. A meadow lark burst into song and was joined by a white-crowned sparrow and a solitaire. The spell was broken. The day and the whole country jumped into wakefulness, vital and alive.

No wonder the old Plains Indians worshipped the sun, for it is the root of all life. They too were aware of this moment in the morning and made a ritual of viewing it from the brow of a hill. The sun was a simple explanation of their existence, their promise of tomorrow and their reassurance of today. For some reason wild animals also sometimes stand motionless at dawn, as though listening to the first soft music of the waking day – caught in the magic. It is a thing to ponder.

A few pages further...

It was mid-June and the middle of the morning high on a sprawling ice field among the Selkirk Mountains of British Columbia. The sun was clear and hot, lighting up a dazzling world among high peaks rearing their fangs like upturned teeth against a brilliant sky, above a rolling sea of mist filling the valley floors to treeline. This is a country where the scale of things is lost in the hugeness and the distance, seeming now like another planet, cut off from the world of men lost in the mist below.

It seemed lifeless too, but then out of a fold in the oceans of snow atop the millenniums of ice, there came a colossal bear – a great boar grizzly. Eight feet he must have been from nose to tail, and weighed perhaps eight hundred pounds. Four weeks out of den, he had burned away most of the left-over fat from the accumulation of the previous season, although he still carried a full winter coat of fur. It was glossy black on his legs and belly, with a bluish silver overcast on his back and flanks that lightened almost to white across his face. His roach was deep, curling forward under his jaw like a beard. His ruff was heavy and thick, almost hiding his dark-colored, rounded ears.

Like a king stalking arrogantly across the raised dais of an immense throne room, he moved in long strides as though he owned the place, which indeed he did; for it was locked away from all but the most venturesome of men. These few were intruders and knew it in their puny efforts to scale these cathedral spires. Like a king he came, made puny too among the towering peaks and glittering blue ice fields, where glaciers spill over cliffs; but he cared not. He was passing through, hungry and possessed of a driving urge. A full twenty miles over high snow he had come since dawn, crossing the range along this ancient bear road, which had no marks and showed no signs of passing except his big, long claw tracks on the slushy surface.

Then he came down across a vast, gently dipping incline to the rim of a great glacial cirque—a snowy bowl carved from solid rock by ages of ice, with one side missing where the valley ran out through a break in the mountains. He stood on the lip of the rim, where a huge snow cornice had broken off, looking down into the head of the Illacillowaet River. His nose was working the warm thermal draft lifting up from the unbroken snow slopes – smells of budding spruces, tumbling waters, wet earth, and many things diluted by the distance smothered in the mist. His urge prodded him. He did not follow the dignity expected of such a one. He spurned the step by step descent, abandoned the role of king and reverted to that of clown; he sat on his broad rump and slid. Going at a speed close to a free fall on the almost perpendicular slope, he skidded sideways and lost his balance but did not care. He went with his tail leading his nose, the wind whistling between his ears. He somersaulted clean over, rolling one way and then the other like a drunken sailor on a greased chute, polishing his belly and then his back. He went on a wind-tearing, joyous plunge, daring catastrophe on the naked rocks below as carefree as a cub, until swallowed up in the mist. Even though the slope was easing, he was still going fifty miles an hour straight for a broken boulder field recently bared by melting snow. The distance to a shattering collision was closing fast, when he came up on his feet in one smooth easy-flowing motion to set his claws and skid to a stop scant feet from the giant boulder. Casually he stepped up on this, once more the regal presence.

Now the wind carried stronger messages for his keen nose to separate and pigeon-hole in their proper mental files. One of these electrified him, and he gave a long sniff that sounded like a wide silk sash being torn sharp and clean in two. He sprang off the boulder and galloped across the broken rock down past the frothing source of a cataract roaring from the bowels of the mountain. He skidded down across wet glacial clay flanking a terminal moraine to hit a faint trail at full speed. It led him down another thousand yards to where the first flower-strewn meadows lay along the mist-shrouded creek.

He paused in a timberline fringe to read the wind again. Out in the middle of a meadow, her magnificent wheat-blond coat glistening with drops of moisture, was a she-grizzly, belly-deep in glacier lilies. . . .

I have mentioned that writers are readers, and Andy Russell, despite being born and raised on a remote ranch in the foothills of Alberta's Rocky Mountains, is no exception. His mother, before her marriage, was a teacher. She brought a good collection of her favorite books to the ranch of her new husband.

Andy, as a boy, read them all of course. In addition, he rode to all the nearby ranches and borrowed their books.

Most importantly, he told me, he read the Bible from cover to cover several times as he was growing up.

As pointed out before, the Bible is chock full of great stories from Jonah and the Big Fish, to Cain and Abel, and to the Prodigal Son. Some universities present a course titled The Bible as Literature.

You should also note that the above excerpt is "non-fiction," but there is no special kind of writing that could be labeled "fiction" or "non-fiction." It is all simply writing – good writing, mediocre writing or awful writing. It took all of Russell's creativeness to fill the blank sheets of paper in the above example, as will your writing regardless of what it is you write for a reader. In any case, I have a difficult time in defining fiction and non-fiction. To me, Steinbeck's *The Grapes of Wrath* is as true as Russell's book on his experiences with Grizzly bears. "Fictionalized Autobiography" may be the best way to describe any kind of writing for a reader.

Note also that Russell gave the Grizzly human characteristics *– the regal presence . . . like a king stalking arrogantly . . . like a drunken sailor*. And what we can probably all relate to, *possessed of a driving urge*.

Putting Elements and Structure Together

The Big IT – a short-short story By A. B. Guthrie, Jr.

Two Plumes was that Injun chief's name. It just hit my mind. Two Plumes, a Piegan, and the place was Fort Benton, Montana Territory, and the time somewheres between 1870 and 1875. I had showed up in the town from over in the Deer Lodge country, lookin' for fun but not for what come.

The place was lively as a hot carcass, for the nabobs from the fur companies had come up from St. Louis, like they did every year, to see how much they'd been cheated out of their legal and honorable earnin's. Steamboats on the levee. Other visitors aplenty in town – bullwackers, muleskinners, prospectors, traders, tinhorn gamblers, crews from the boats, new crop of girls, all bein' merry.

And to boot, there was a big bunch of Injuns, mostly Piegans, but Bloods, too, and other kinds I didn't savvy. A passel, I tell you. Their tepees was pitched out a ways, God knows why, for mornin', noon and night they hung around town.

People was a little ticklish, seein' the Injuns was so many. Give them savages some little excuse, they said between hiccups and rumpuses, and they might forget their manners, which wasn't high-toned at the best.

Then, from some tradin' post, a pack train showed up. Tied on one of the mules, with muzzle pointn' the same way as the mule's was a little brass cannon, or what they call a mountain howitzer.

It took a little time to see that here was the big IT. The trouble with opportunity is that its name's written on its butt. Fire that canon, the smart somebody said. Make boom. Make goddamn big hole in far bluff of river. Show Injuns real medicine. Scare devil out of red devils.

There wasn't no argument on that motion. It had just to be put to get a unanimous vote. So the boys went out to round up the Injuns, tellin' by tongue and by sign to come see the big show. Meantime some others said they' cut the mule from the string and plant him close to the river. Them with no special duties kept circulatin', makin' sure that all hands was informed.

Everyone was, Injun and white. The Injuns came in a herd, in blankets and buckskins and bare skins, and so did the whites, all of 'em includin' some ladies not so damn ladylike they couldn't enjoy theirselves. You never seen such a crowd.

Like now, of course, Front Street was half-faced, buildin's on one side, river on t'other. The mule men had led the mule to the shore. On yon side was a cut bank they figured would make a good target. The rest of us pushed around close, makin' a kind of a half circle, the heathens composin' one horn of it and us redeemers the other, though there was some mixin' up, it bein' hard to remember it was them that needed to see and get educated.

Now in the front row of the Injuns I spotted this old chief, Two Plumes, that I had smoked with a time or two. He had his arms folded and the look on his face that a redskin can wear which says nothin' will ever surprise him, in particular white men and their doin's. The other bucks was wearin' it too. You can't beat an Injun for lookin' like he wouldn't let on that you stink.

The men with the mule got the cannon loaded, one standin' on a box so's to get at the muzzle and feed it a whole hatful of powder and then poke the ball home.

So then all was ready save for the sightin'. Aimin' the piece meant aimin' the mule first and then seein' to the refinements. Wasn't no trouble. That sleepy old mule was agreeable. He led around and whoad with tail dead on the target and went back to sleep. With one man at his head another climbed up and squinted over the barrel and fiddled with doodads and got down, claimin' the piece was trained finer than frog hair.

The ramrod of this frolic, whoever he was, made a little speech then, tellin' the Injuns to look-see across far water where the whiteman's terrible medicine iron would blow the dust tall. With that, he turned to his terrible crew. "Ready?" he said.

They sighted again and nodded for yes, and he told 'em "Fire away, Men!"

One of 'em touched a match to the fuse.

The fuse fizzed and fizzed, and Mister Mule opened one eye and then both, and he flapped his ears back and let out a snort while the crew hollered whoa and hung hard to his head. Huh-uh! The mule hunched a hump in his back and began buck-jumpin' around in a wheel, the cannon bobbin' its big eye at one and another of all of us innocent bystanders while the fuse et down toward the charge.

For a shake no one could move, but just for a shake. Me, I found myself lyin' behind a scatter of driftwood, and some feller was tryn' to scratch under me like a mole praying: "No! Don't shoot! No!" to the mule.

That feller tunneled me up over my fort. The mule was wheelin' and the fuse fusn' and the cannon pickin' up targets, and them innocent targets, I tell you, was wild on the wing or dead flat on the ground or neckdeep in the river, duckin' like hell-divers when the muzzle swung around. But the Injuns stood still, waitin' for the tall dust to blow.

Then, like a close clap of thunder, the cannon went off!

It didn't hurt anything. What with the mule's jumpin', it had slid back, down the slope of his rump, so's the ball skimmed his tail and went into the ground.

Men began comin' from cover and trailin' up in the dust and the powder smoke, smilin' pale and damn silly.

I walked over to Two Plumes, who was standin' with his arms folded like before, with nothin' in his face that showed anything.

"How," I said. "How chief like 'im?"

He answered, "How?" and let the rest of it wait, but in that Injun eye was a gleam. Then he said, "Paleface jackass poop."

As you can see, this story has all the elements – characters, conflict, suspense, change. And it fits perfectly into the dramatic form – opening at a tense moment of change; characters in conflict; then downhill as background is filled in. Rising action as mule is loaded with gun and powder; the climax as mule bucks; gun swings about; people dive for cover. Finally the denouement when gun fires into the ground, confirming for the Indians what they already suspected about the White Man.

Put Some Poetry In It

From *A River Runs Through It* – By Norman Maclean

When Maclean was writing this series of stories, he took the first stories to a writing friend, and she told him to "put some poetry in it." In this excerpt, we will find how well he took her advice.

Maclean described this book as "fictionalized autobiography" which I think is a good description of ALL so-called creative writing.

This excerpt is from "The Cook, and a Hole in the Sky" and relates Maclean's experiences as a youth working for the U.S. Forest Service in Montana. At this time, the forest service had no fire lookout towers – simply a young man camped out on top of a mountain with an alidade – a tool for measuring direction – and a telephone.

As well as metaphor, strong verbs and details, watch for rhythm and emotion.

In the late afternoon, of course, the mountains meant all business for the lookouts. The big winds were veering from the valleys toward the peaks, and smoke from little fires that had been secretly burning for several days might show up for the first time. New fires sprang out of thunder before it sounded. By three-thirty or four, the lightning would be flexing itself on the distant ridges like a fancy prizefighter, skipping sideways, ducking, showing off but not hitting anything. By four-thirty or five, it was another game. You could feel the difference in the air that had become hard to breathe. The lightning now came walking into you, delivering short smashing punches. With an alidade, you marked a line on the map toward where it had struck and started counting, "thousand-one, thousand-two" and so on, putting in the "thousand" to slow your count to a second each time. If the thunder reached you at "thousand-five," you figured the lightning had struck about a mile away. The punches became shorter and the count closer and you knew you were going to take punishment. Then the lightning and thunder struck together. There was no count.

But what I remember best is crawling out of the tent on summer nights when on high mountains autumn is always approaching. To a boy it is something new and beautiful to piss among the stars. Not under the stars but among them. Even at night great winds seem always to blow on great mountains, and tops of trees bend, but, as the boy stands there with nothing to do but to watch, seemingly the sky itself bends and the stars blow down through the trees until the Milky Way becomes lost in some distant forest. As the cosmos brushes by the boy and disappears among the trees, the sky is continually replenished with stars. There would be stars enough to brush by him all night, but by now the boy is getting cold.

Then the shivering organic speck of steam itself disappears.
WOW !

Maclean was 70 when he wrote this, his first book, after spending his adult years as an English professor at the University of Chicago.

Is It True or Did You Make It Up?

Foreword to *Collected Stories of Wallace Stegner*

It would not be accurate to say that these stories gathered up near the end of a lifetime of writing constitute an autobiography, even a fragmentary one. I have tried autobiography and found that I am not to be trusted with it. I hate the restrictiveness of facts, I can't control my impulse to rearrange, suppress, add, heighten, invent, and improve. Accuracy means less to me than suggestiveness; my memory is as much an inventor as a recorder, and when it has operated in these stories it has operated almost as freely as if no personal history were involved.

Nevertheless the thirty-one stories in this volume do make a sort of personal record. I lived them, either as participant or spectator or auditor before I made fictions of them. Because I have a tyrannous sense of place, they are laid in places that I know well – many of them in Saskatchewan, where I spent my childhood, and in Salt Lake City, where I misspent my youth, and in California, where I have lived for forty-five years, and in Vermont, where I have spent at least part of the last fifty summers. I have written about the kind of people I know, in the places where I have known them. If art is a by-product of living, and I believe it is, then I want my own efforts to stay as close to earth and human experience as possible – and the only earth I know is the one I have lived on, the only human experience I am at all sure of is my own . . .

Still More Scene Writing

From *The Education of a Badlands Boy*
– By Ken Lewis

While I was not to have an academic life, I was to have a far more fundamental one. My curiosity and the difficulties in satisfying it from books forced me to turn to nature. "Forced" is not the right word. "Allowed" is the right one, for what better teacher to learn from and what better subject to study?

And what better schoolhouse than the prairies and badlands, mountains and streams of Western South Dakota?

I retain vivid vignettes of this time.

My earliest memory finds me squatting beside a puddle miraculously appearing in a field from the snow melt and Spring rains. The water is clear with a tinge of tea coloring from the drowned plants; the sweet smell of green, growing prairie grass mixes with the musty smell of damp earth and the pungent smell of rotting debris. The pond's edge, where I squat, bursts with life darting about to complete the business of reproduction before hot, prairie winds turns the water to cracked earth and the grasses to brittle brown. Strings of milky frog semen drift about like sputum; the clear, tapioca-size bubbles of frog eggs clump around grass stems, most fertilized, with the black dot in the center already growing. A huge dragon fly nymph crawls slowly along the bottom. They can bite, I knew, and the skittering water bugs are too fast to catch.

Frogs, silenced by my coming, start up their mating cacophony of far-carrying croaks and bird-like chirps, and the mosquitoes are biting, intent also on reproduction using blood siphoned from the back of my neck for their needs.

I quickly discovered frogs do not make good pets. You put them in your pocket, and when you take them out they have (forgive me) croaked – their wet skin, source of their oxygen, dried.

Snakes are much better.

During the summers, I always had a snake. They loved it in the dark and warmth of my pocket, and they loved me. A baby garter snake strikes and tries to bite when you catch it, but it quickly becomes tame and coils in the palm of your hand as you gently stroke its silky skin.

Even in those days an occasional tourist would stop in at the Wall Drug Store, and I remember one of Wall's adults calling out to me on the street:

"Hey, Kenny, come over here and show the lady your snake."

She giggled at the man's attempt at humor. But he knew, as did everyone in Wall, that I would have a snake in my pocket.

I pulled it out. She stopped grinning and quickly got into her car.

I can imagine her story when she got back to Chicago, or wherever she was from:

"We stopped in this funny little town in the Badlands where every little boy has a snake in his pocket."

A Note to Teachers

Of course, no one has had the same experiences as I have as a professional writer and as a teacher of writing. Consequently I do not expect anyone to follow the suggestions in this guide "out the window," as the saying goes. Consider the ideas here as starting points in your thinking as you organize your class around the textbook.

Grading is one of the first things many students think about, so that might be a good place to start. I wish there were no grades in a course such as this, but one has to consider the institution's policy and the students' expectations.

I explain to the students that "those who come to class, study the textbook and do the assignments conscientiously can expect an A or a B – most likely an A. How can I evaluate the quality of your work? Should I rate your writing against John Steinbeck's, for example? Having come to class, studied and written ensures that you will have learned, and that's the point.

"Those who 'kiss off' the assignments can expect a C. Those who do something will get a D and those who do nothing, an F."

As you can see, evaluating a student's creative work is a problem. What standard can you apply? If you gave a student's paper an A for its quality, what grade would you give Steinbeck?

It seems to me that the worse thing a teacher can do is use a red pencil and mark all the grammar and spelling errors. That's not what story writing is all about. As I explain to students: "This is not an English course. What you learn here applies equally well to writing a story in Swahili." (I always hoped a student would turn in an assignment in Swahili, but none ever has.)

For me, the best way of evaluating is one-to-one. I find that it takes little more time to meet with each student individually and go over the assignment than for me to read through their work and write down my comments. After assignments are turned in, and I have a chance to glance through them, I schedule each student for a 10-minute session in my office. (I hand out a one-day time sheet divided into 10-minute periods and each student picks the time period that fits into his or her schedule.)

To me, an assignment handed back marked with red pencil can be discouraging and does little to help a student improve. In a one-to-one session your comments and observations can all be encouraging and supportive, even though they might cover the same points as the red marks that you would have put on the paper.

I think comments should be general and supportive for the most part, although specific suggestions for improvement are also in order. But not too much of that. Criticism, I feel, does little to help students learn to write well. They must learn to criticize and evaluate their own work – with a bit of help from you.

Now to the nitty-gritty – the assignments.

The first assignment is to have the students read the book from cover to cover. No big deal. Most should be able to get through it in several hours.

Next, students should be required to study chapters 6, 7 and 8 and then write a descriptive scene – some place they are very familiar with and for which they have some emotional feeling. It could be anything from a farm field to a city street or a mountain. Steinbeck's *The Turtle* in the Appendix should be their model. They should be advised to relax, have fun and use strong verbs, metaphors and "little particulars" in their scene which should be about one page long, double-spaced with normal margins.

It's been my experience that about half the boys will want to write science-fiction, and half the girls fantasy. They should be forbidden to do this, explaining that if they really want to write in those genres, they can take what they learn in this class and apply it to that kind of story later. In this class, they will be writing what they know, and to some degree, from their own experience. The reason students want to write science-fiction or fantasy is two-fold – one, they believe it allows them to be uninvolved in the story, and two, they don't have to reveal anything about themselves. These feelings are understandable, but they are LEARNING to be writers. Writers must become emotionally involved in their stories, and writers must develop the courage to reveal their innermost thoughts and feelings.

Next, students should be required to study chapters 9, 13, 16 and 17, and add to their descriptive scene two characters in a scene of conflict using mainly dialogue to reveal the characters and reveal what is going on. The scene should be three or four pages long, and students can be given some time to do this. While they are working on this scene, they can read their descriptive paragraphs in class, while you make sure each student is well-complimented.

You can also use this time to review the book, in general, and to explain that the students will be "building" a story, starting with a descriptive scene; then introducing characters and conflict; followed by writing a plot narrative; and finally writing an opening scene to fit into plot narrative. Explain that this opening scene should contain all the elements – establish time and place, introduce the main character or characters, and suggest the problem.

This scene should be polished again and again, keeping in mind all the instructions in writing opening scenes in chapter 21 – "striking the keynote at once" – and determining point of view and voice as explained in chapters 19 and 20 – this assignment could be considered the "final exam."

You might wish to explain to students that the idea for a story may come from any place, and that writers each have their own way of working. However, at some point most of them will begin "building" a story as students have done in this class, although many writers may not necessarily do this "building" on a conscious level. As reading assignments, students could be required to read Steinbeck's *The Pearl* and *Of Mice and Men*, and to identify each of the parts of the dramatic form in these stories.

I feel class time should be spent in reading students' work, and in far-ranging discussions on the art and craft of writing, particularly those examples in the Appendix where the "nuts and bolts" are illustrated by the Masters. One of the aspects of learning to write, I firmly believe, is learning to read and evaluate one's own writing.

In the end, I don't know how many students will become famous writers of literature, but "the story" elements will be useful to them for any kind of writing, from Harlequin romances to essays to journalism to letters. As I say in the book: "The mind is a wonderful instrument. It can learn by tearing down and analyzing, and create by putting together, in its own way, what it has learned."

Notes

Notes

Notes

Notes

Notes

Notes

Notes